Primer on Workers' Compensation

Second Edition

PRIMER ON WORKERS' COMPENSATION

Second Edition

Jeffrey V. Nackley

The Bureau of National Affairs, Inc., Washington, D.C.

Library of Congress Cataloging-in-Publication Data

Nackley, Jeffrey V.
Primer on workers' compensation/Jeffrey V. Nackley.—2nd ed. p. cm.

Bibliography: p.
Includes index.
ISBN 0-87179-596-5
1. Workers' compensation—Law and legislation—United States—States. I. Title.
KF3615.Z95N33 1989
344.73'021—dc19
[347.30421] 89-31139
CIP

Published by BNA Books,
1231 25th St., N.W., Washington, D.C. 20037

Printed in the United States of America
International Standard Book Number: 0-87179-596-5

For my sister and for Dee Graham Gallon

INTRODUCTION

A primer on workers' compensation? Covering the provisions of fifty states, a half dozen more territories and commonwealths, a couple of federal workers' compensation acts, all of them different and none simple. The project seemed initially undoable; yet in over a decade in this field I've come to see that there are issues in workers' compensation that cut across all boundaries. Even though the different laws and regulations may provide different answers, the questions and the basic vocabulary are the same throughout the country.

This book is not meant to be comprehensive. Now in its second edition, this book serves as an introduction to the field of workers' compensation. It is also designed as an overview of our compensation systems. In this sense, I hope it will furnish perspectives that will be useful to professionals already involved in the field in their particular roles, as insurers, government administrators, judges, actuaries, union representatives, physicians, psychologists, rehabilitation workers, and lawmakers, not to mention employers, injured workers, teachers, lawyers, and writers.

The book's nine chapters provide an overview of the vocabulary and basic concepts underlying workers' compensation claims and benefits (chapters 1-5) and the administration and procedures involved in operating workers' compensation systems and providing benefits (chapters 6-9). Specifically, this second edition includes recent changes in statutory and case law, and expanded discussions of mental stress claims and temporary partial disability awards, settlements, and stipulations. The appendices contain 1989 summaries of the various jurisdictions' statutory provisions, as well as current addresses and telephone numbers of the various workers' compensation administrative offices.

Selecting legal citations for a book like this presented a special problem. I have tried to be flexible with sources, using them at times to give examples of majority views or of positions taken in the text of the book, at other times to show differing or minority views, and at still other times merely to give the reader what I view as the best general source to begin in-depth research.

I'm overdue on several debts of thanks to the members of the staff of BNA Books—particularly Louise Goines—for their encouragement and support in the writing of both editions of the *Primer*.

The debt is also overdue to Debbie Cumberland of the U.S. Chamber of Commerce who has cooperated completely with me and with BNA Books in making available the valuable charts from the Chamber's *Analysis*. The charts represent exhaustive work by the Chamber and provide a unique addition to the *Primer*.

Finally, Nancy Moran has provided excellent copy editing of the manuscripts and went far beyond her assignment in giving the book criticism and sympathetic readings.

Jeffrey V. Nackley

Washington, D.C.
March 1989

CONTENTS

1
OVERVIEW

Workers' compensation is a system—or more accurately, is the label given to many systems in various jurisdictions of the United States and other countries—by which individuals who sustain physical or mental injuries due to their jobs are compensated for their disabilities, medical costs, and, on some occasions, for the costs of their rehabilitation, and by which the survivors or workers who are killed receive compensation for lost financial support. In the United States, state workers' compensation laws cover most workers who are not covered by federal programs. Federal coverage is provided exclusively by the Longshore and Harborworkers' Compensation Act, which applies to maritime workers on the navigable waters of the United States, and by the Federal Employees' Compensation Act, which applies to the civilian employees of the U.S. government. Otherwise, federal law has little direct bearing on workers' compensation law.

Historically, workers' compensation came into being in the late 19th and early 20th centuries, when the Industrial Revolution brought sweeping changes in the workplace. The number and severity of injuries increased, and traditional theories of recovery in tort and contract law were found to be cumbersome, unfair, and wholly inadequate to the task of charging industry with the economic costs of the human injury it caused.

Although there are as many different workers' compensation systems as there are jurisdictions, some characteristics are fairly general. Most systems, for example, have well-differentiated types of claims, types of compensation, conditions for coverage, kinds of insurance coverage available, and provisions for employers' protection. In addition, some basic definitions and certain concepts regarding administration and procedures are common to the various systems, whether federal or state. A description of these common aspects of workers' compensation systems may be helpful to everyone connected with the field and is provided below. Discussions of specific state and federal workers' compensation programs can be found in publications listed in the Bibliography.

TYPES OF CLAIMS

A workers' compensation claim is an application by an individual, under a state or federal program, for compensation and other benefits for a medical condition that resulted from work. Most states differentiate among injury or accident claims, occupational disease claims, and death claims. Some states also provide for separate safety-code-violation claims.

A claim is sometimes said to be certified or recognized by an employer when the employer has not contested it and allowed or disallowed (or denied) by a state agency when the employer has contested it. The mere fact that the employer fails to contest a claim does not mean that the insurance carrier is bound to pay on the claim; it usually means that the employer and employee agree on factual questions. As a practical matter, however, such claims are usually allowed by the workers' compensation administrative agency.

Injury or Accident Claims

The most common type of workers' compensation claims, these are traditionally defined as claims for disabilities that have resulted from "accidents," i.e., sudden, traumatic, and unexpected incidents.

The classic everyday "accident," an automobile collision, has all these characteristics. Obviously similar incidents include falls, trips, and traumas resulting from mishaps with tools (hammers, saws) or machines. Other sorts of incidents such as strains of the back from lifting heavy objects are said to be only accidental "in effect," since there is nothing unusual about the cause of the accident. In some systems, the cause of the injury must be "accidental" for the incident to be compensable; in others the effect must be "accidental"; in still others, both or neither cause and effect must be "accidental."

For a detailed discussion of accident or injury claims, see Chapter 2.

Occupational Disease Claims

This category includes claims for disabilities resulting from various ailments that are associated with particular industrial trades or processes. They may be funded separately from injury claims but sometimes are neither separately defined nor separately funded.

Many diseases have historically been recognized to be connected to certain occupations. Occupational disease programs are designed to charge the costs of such diseases to the industry that produces them rather than to the individual victim or to society at large (in the form of welfare or insurance costs). Common occupational diseases include coal miners' pneumoconiosis or "black lung disease," silicosis, and asbestosis and other asbestos-related conditions.

For further discussion, see Chapter 3.

Distinctions Between Injuries and Occupational Diseases

Most systems provide a separate definition for occupational disease, even if it is considered a subcategory of "injury." Wyoming's workers' compensation law, for example, which contains no separate definition for occupational diseases, contains an extremely general definition of "injury" and includes occupational disease in that definition by creating an exception to an exception of that definition.

In Alaska, California, Hawaii, Massachusetts, and Wisconsin, however, there is no real distinction between those medical conditions that result from a single incident and those that result from exposure to industrial hazards. The same is true of the federal workers' compensation acts—the Longshore and Harborworkers' Compensation Act and the Federal Employees' Compensation Act.

Death Claims

Death claims are applications for benefits made most often by surviving family members of individuals who have been killed in the course of employment or who have died as the result of work-related accidents or occupational diseases. Benefits payable on an allowed claim are usually periodic direct payments to a surviving spouse, dependent children, or other dependent family members; funeral expenses; and medical bills for the last illness.

For further discussion, see Chapter 4.

Safety-code Violations

Safety codes and the effect of violations of such codes on claims vary widely from state to state. Some industrial states, such as Ohio, provide for a claim for an additional award to the claimant which is assessed directly against the employer if an injury, occupational disease, or death results from violation of a safety code by the employer. Michigan is an example of an industrial state that makes no special provision for safety-code-violation claims.

TYPES OF COMPENSATION

Most jurisdictions provide compensation to disabled workers under similar categories: temporary total disability, temporary partial disability (wage impairments or impairments in earning capacity), permanent partial disability, permanent total disability, and scheduled losses. In addition, many plans provide for change-of-occupation awards. Under certain allowed workers' compensation claims, which are usually referred to as "medical only" claims, medical bills are paid but *no* direct payments are made to the injured worker.

For further discussion, see Chapter 5.

TYPES OF JOBS COVERED

In most states, workers' compensation coverage is compulsory for any employer with a minimum number of workers, but it is nominally elective in South Carolina and Texas, both of which provide significant economic risk for an employer who chooses not to insure. Wyoming requires coverage for "hazardous" employments and permits coverage for nonhazardous employments. In many states, employers of less than a specified number of employees (the highest minimum is five) are not required to obtain coverage and, hence, their workers are unprotected.

The general rule is the workers' compensation covers only employees. Independent contractors or lessees, or individuals in non-employment relationships with a principal, are not covered. Casual employees and domestic workers who earn less than a specified amount per calendar quarter also are not usually covered by workers' compensation. State workers' compensation systems do not cover workers who come within federal jurisdiction, such as interstate railroad workers, maritime workers, and federal employees. Separate federal statutes provide coverage for these individuals.

COVERAGE

Employers within the workers' compensation system (sometimes referred to as "amenable employers") must comply with workers' compensation law by either obtaining insurance or, where permitted, insuring themselves. Although workers are usually covered by operation of law even if an employer has failed to obtain coverage, noncomplying employers are subject to various penalties, typically including loss of certain common-law defenses in a lawsuit by injured workers for negligence or other tort, fines, liability for back premium (even if no protection for the employer is granted), liability for workers' compensation claims on a dollar-for-dollar basis, and criminal penalties.

There are three basic options available to employers seeking workers' compensation coverage: state-fund insurance, private insurance, and self-insurance.

State-fund Coverage

In a limited number of states, private insurance of workers' compensation is not permitted. Instead, employers are required to subscribe to a monopolistic state fund, a system that is generally regarded as highly efficient financially, although sometimes hampered by bureaucratic delays in making payments in even uncontested claims. Most states with monopolistic state funds permit large employers to self-insure. Other states with competitive state-run funds allow the private insurance of workers' compensation risks.

Private Insurance Coverage

In the majority of states that permit private insurance of workers' compensation, an employer may choose from among various insurance carriers.

Self-insurance

The third option typically available to employers is self-insurance. Large employers, usually upon the depositing of a surety bond, are permitted to pay directly the claims filed by their own workers and are given a great deal of discretion in administering their own risks. Self-insurance is sometimes referred to as a "privilege," particularly in those states that do not permit private insurance. Self-insured employers are required to pay to their workers the same benefits as workers would receive under the state fund or private insurance. For practical as well as strategic reasons, most large employers find it beneficial to self-insure as soon as feasible.

For a breakdown of the various types of coverage permitted in jurisdictions of the United States, see U.S. Chamber of Commerce Chart, "Coverage of Laws," Appendix A.

ADMINISTRATION AND PROCEDURES

Administrative functions of workers' compensation programs may be broadly divided into overseeing and/or disbursing funds and conducting hearings for the resolution of both disputed claims and insurance issues. Accordingly, bureaus, boards of agency appeals, or industrial commissions usually administer programs, and, in some instances, two state agencies handle the functions separately, one agency to oversee and/or disburse, and the other to resolve conflicts. These state agencies often have concurrent jurisdiction over claims, with the adjudicating board having superior power. In a few states, courts administer the programs.

Notice of injury, death, occupational disease, or safety-code violation usually must be given to either the employer or the state agency. In some states, notice is given separately from filing a claim; in others, filing a claim with a state agency or with an employer fills all the notice requirements of the statute. In those jurisdictions requiring separate notice to the employer, the notice period is typically quite short—30 days, for example—but may be waived. In states requiring only the filing of a claim as notice, the notice period is, of course, the same as the statute of limitations, which is often as long as 2 years. These statutes of limitations frequently are not subject to waiver of any kind.

Evidence rules for workers' compensation administrative hearings are greatly modified from those applied in courts, and the scope of judicial review is often narrow. Court review generally is limited to determinations of whether the administrative agencies abused their discretion, made factual findings without evidentiary support, or made an error of law. In those few states that permit *de novo* review in court, the court rules of civil procedure usually obtain, but the appealable issues are often limited to allowance of claims or of medical conditions. Chapters 6 and 7 provide more detailed discussions of the administration of and the procedures applicable to workers' compensation claims.

EMPLOYERS' RIGHTS AND PROTECTIONS

In exchange for paying workers' compensation premiums or for obtaining the right or privilege to self-insure, the employer receives immunity from lawsuit. This means that it cannot be sued for its negligence that results in a compensable claim. The immunity, however, does not necessarily protect the employer from being sued for its intentional actions that result in personal injury to its workers. In cases alleging intentional action by the employer—an area of law that is changing—the questions raised would include whether the intentional act of the employer removed the injury or the employee from the course of employment, and the degree of fault attributable to the employer's intentional action. Some cases have definitely said that the employer may be sued for any action that it was reasonably certain would result in injury to the employee. Employers' rights and protections are also discussed in Chapter 9.

POLICY CONSIDERATIONS AND RULES OF CONSTRUCTION

Workers' compensation is considered a beneficial system and remedial in character. Accordingly, it is liberally construed in favor of the intended beneficiaries. Liberal construction does not mean that courts are free to deviate from plainly stated legislation but it does mean that ambiguities in statutes will be resolved in favor of coverage and that otherwise valid claims will not be denied on the basis of technicalities.

Even though workers' compensation is a "new" field of law, in the sense that it did not exist in the common law that the United States received from England and in fact only came into being in the early 20th century by statute, liberal construction of workers' compensation laws is widely accepted. Some early cases such as *Andrejwski v. Wolverine Coal Co.*, in which the Michigan Supreme Court held that workers' compensation statutes are to be strictly construed as being in "derogation" of common law, can only be regarded as historical oddities.

The usual rules of interpreting statutes apply to workers' compensation laws as well, and the underlying purpose of the law, that is, to compensate injured and diseased workers and the dependents of killed workers in as expeditious and non-adversarial a manner as possible, can aid courts in construing workers' compensation provisions. Other aids to statutory construction include interpretations of a particular statute by the agency or agencies charged with administering it, and interpretations of similar statutes by courts of other jurisdictions.

2

Injuries and Accidents

The most common type of worker's compensation claim is the injury or accident claim. Historically, worker's compensation provided coverage for claims based on "accidents," which were often described as sudden, unexpected, or out-of-the-ordinary occurrences. Montana's definition of "a tangible happening of a traumatic nature from an unexpected cause or unusual strain resulting in either external or internal physical harm and such physical condition as a result therefrom and excluding disease not traceable to injury" is an elaborate articulation of the traditional view of a covered accident.

Although the requirements that an injury must be sudden, unusual, or not in the usual course of events appear gradually to be giving way, it nevertheless remains true that injuries must be "unexpected" in the sense that they are unintended. In general, "injuries" no longer need be "accidents" in the sense that, say, an automobile collision is an accident, but they must still be "accidental" in the sense that the injured party did not intend the injurious result. Self-inflicted injuries and injuries caused by third parties will be discussed later in this chapter, and an employer's tort liability for injuries caused by its intentional acts will be discussed in Chapter 9, which deals with the issue of employer immunity.

In some states, detailed descriptions of accidents were given for the specific purpose of distinguishing them from occupational diseases, which were often either excluded from coverage or included only in separate funding schemes and subject to stricter conditions for coverage or for benefits. However, the gradual erosion of the old requirements for compensability of injuries—suddenness, unusualness, and departure from the ordinary course of events—implies that the distinction between injuries and occupational diseases also is collapsing, even in those jurisdictions whose statutes retain the legal distinction. Hence, in some cases, the main question to be addressed in a claim will be simply whether or not a particular disability was caused by employment.

Both injuries and diseases must be work-related in order to be compensable. This generally means that they must in fact be caused by the employment. But for each coverage category, the concept has more specific definitions.

WORK-RELATED INJURIES

The terms "in the course of employment" and "arising out of employment" occur again and again in workers' compensation law and are typical but certainly not universal standards by which injuries are determined to be work-related. In those jurisdictions that use the terms in their statutes or in controlling judicial cases, it may be said that if an accident or injury is found to be "in the course of and arising out of employment" then it is, by definition, work-related. Conversely, it is sometimes said that being "in the course of and arising out of employment" is nothing more or less than cause in fact, i.e., work-relatedness.

The quite logical suggestion has therefore been made that use of the terms "in the course of and arising out of employment" only adds confusion to the law and that the question should be, and usually has been, whether or not an injury, disease, or bodily condition was work-related, i.e., whether it was caused by the employment.

Some jurisdictions have adopted this approach and treat as compensable all bodily conditions that were caused by employment. The result, however, has not been significantly different from those jurisdictions that adhere to the traditional "in the course of and arising out of employment" approach. A

Texas appellate court in *Texas Employers' Ins. Ass'n v. Dean* faced with the problem of an injury occurring in the employer's parking lot reached a similar conclusion using reasoning similar to that of a New Jersey court dealing with the same issue in *Thornton v. Chamberlain Mfg. Co.*, even though the two states have quite different definitions of "injury." Both courts allowed the claims.

In other words, it appears that as a general rule, the traditional terms "in the course of" and "arising out of employment" mean simply that an injury was caused by work and, regardless of the statutory language used, define when an injury is compensable.

IN THE COURSE OF AND ARISING OUT OF EMPLOYMENT

Although these two operative terms contained in the phrase, "in the course of and arising out of employment," are often treated as though they had merged into one relatively simple concept, namely, whether an injury was in fact caused by employment, certain situations often require courts to examine or reexamine one or the other separately.

In the Course of Employment

Inquiry into whether an injury occurred "in the course of employment" is one way of asking whether the time and the place of the injury bore a close enough connection to employment to render it fairly and rationally chargeable to the compensation system. Normally, injuries occurring at work are so obviously work-connected in time and place that the question does not even occur to anyone. (In such instances, if work-relatedness is in dispute, the usual question is whether the injury "arose out of" the employment.) But interesting workers' compensation problems arise when injuries occur to employees in the following circumstances:

- Employees who are engaged in some errand or activity not directly connected with work but giving some subsidiary benefit to employment, e.g., while taking a class or while participating in sporting events, for the purpose of increasing their value as employees.

It's difficult to fashion a general rule in these cases. Differing results have been reached in similar circumstances. The New Jersey Supreme Court in *Strezelecki v. Johns-Manville Products Corp.*, for example, allowed a claim for a death that occurred when an employee was involved in an automobile accident on his way to study for university classes that his employer paid for and that were in furtherance of his career as a financial analyst in his employment. On the other hand, the Florida Supreme Court in *Mathias v. South Daytona* disallowed a claim for an injury sustained by a police officer during a softball game in which he was strongly encouraged to participate. There is no good rule of thumb for making sense out of the varying results in this category of injuries.

- Employees at an employment-sponsored function away from the regular situs of work, e.g., picnic, dinner, party.

These injuries are generally recognized as being in the course of employment and compensable, particularly if the employee was compelled, either directly or indirectly, to attend. The dispositive question in such cases, whether the employer derived some benefit from the affair, is usually answered in the affirmative; the Rhode Island Supreme Court's decision of *Beauchesne v. David London & Co.*, allowing a claim of an employee who sustained a severe injury when he became drunk at a company Christmas party, cannot really be considered aberrant.

On those occasions when a claim in this category is disallowed, the reasons usually given are that it was not clear whether the employer actually sponsored the event, as in *Chilton v. Gray School of Medicine* (N.C.), or that employer's sponsorship was so minimal that it received no substantial benefit from the function, as in *Pasko v. Beecher Co.* (Minn.).

Nevada's workers' compensation law specifically excludes injuries sustained at a social gathering unless the workers are paid, while the California code states that voluntary participation in off-duty sports events is not covered. Ohio now permits employees to waive coverage for injuries or disabilities incurred while participating voluntarily in employer-sponsored recreation or fitness activities.

- Employees such as traveling salesmen who have no fixed situs of employment, or workers who operate from their home. The general rule in such cases is easy: Injuries are compensable whenever the individual is performing work for the employer. It is more difficult to determine when the work begins and when it ends in particular situations.
- Employees whose work requires some entertainment of customers or clients so that the distinction between situs of work and situs of personal activities is unclear.

Again, the general rule is deceptively simple: Employees engaged in work for the employer are "in the course of" their employment. Courts generally allow compensation if there is a sufficiently close connection between the entertaining and the employee's work, *Shunk v. Gulf American Land Corp.* (Fla.), *Green v. Heard Motor Co.* (La.), *Harrison v. Stanton* (N.J.). But factual inquiries into this question are often extremely difficult and courts often resort to liberal construction of workers' compensation law as an aid in its resolution.

- Employees engaged in some personal activity while on the employer's premises during work hours.

The central question in such cases is usually phrased, was the act purely in the employee's interest or was it incidental to employment? But divergent results have been reached on the same facts. Some indication of the varying views possible in these cases was expressed in *Leckie v. H.D. Foote Lumber Co.* by a Louisiana appeals court that, after reconsideration, reversed itself and denied compensation to a lumber-mill employee who was injured while sawing a piece of scrap lumber for his personal use.

Relevant factors in resolving this issue include

whether the injury took place during regular work hours, whether stand-by or idle time is part of the nature of the job, and whether the employee's engaging in such personal activity was known by the employer and whether it was permitted or prohibited.

Factual variations are so wide in this category that only a few examples will be given here. The North Carolina Supreme Court denied compensation to a watchman for an injury he sustained while washing his car *(Bell v. Dewey Bros., Inc.)*; a department-store employee was held by the Ohio Supreme Court not to be in the course of employment while making a purchase of articles for himself "on company time" *(Industrial Commission of Ohio v. Ahern)*; a service-station operator who was injured while repairing his own car at work was granted compensation by the Nebraska Supreme Court *(Chrisman v. Farmers Cooperative Ass'n)*; a laundry employee's injuries sustained while pressing a skirt for a co-worker after working hours were held to be not compensable by the Tennessee Supreme Court *(Hinton Laundry Co. v. De Lozier)*.

Arising Out of Employment

At this point, it should become clearer that asking whether an injury was sustained "in the course of employment" is simply one aspect of the question whether an injury was caused by employment. In those categories of fact situations discussed above, it is easier to approach that question by asking whether the injury was sustained "in the course of employment."

It is a relatively arbitrary decision to analyze one fact category, for example, injuries sustained while an employee is engaged in personal activity during business hours, under the "in the course of employment" approach rather than the "arising out of employment" language. Under the former, one would ask whether the personal activity removed the worker from "the course of employment." Under the latter, one would ask whether the injury arose out of the individual's work rather than out of his personal activity. The basic question, whether the injury was caused by work, and the answer should be the same under both approaches.

The following categories of claims illustrate this point. The usefulness—let alone the analytical validity—of distinguishing "course of employment" from "arising out of employment" more or less disintegrates, and it is best in these "arising out of employment" cases to keep only the ultimate question in mind: Did the employment cause the injury?

- Employees who are away from the site of employment but are on standby or on call for work.

  The general rule is that if an individual is injured performing a duty of work or is injured because of a risk incurred because of the job, the injury is compensable. An on-call management employee who was ordered by his employer to keep the plant in operation during a labor strike and who was beaten and called a "dirty scab" when he stepped out of his car at his residence was held to have suffered a compensable injury in the New Jersey case of *Meo v. Commercial Can Corp.* Some cases, like *Haugen v. State Accident Ins. Fund* (Or.) and *Kelly v. County of Nassau* (N.Y.), put the rule conversely: Injuries sustained while performing work voluntarily or for the benefit of the employee rather than of the employer are not compensable.
- Individuals who are required to live on the employer's premises and are injured while performing some personal activity.

  The general rule is that injuries are compensable if incurred in the performance of work duties or reasonably attributable or incidental to the conditions under which such an employee lives. Exceptions to this general rule of compensability are usually explained by an employee's not being required to live on employer's premises but living there voluntarily, as in, for example, *Guiliano v. Daniel O'Connell's Sons* (Conn.), *Kraft v. West Hotel Co.* (Iowa), and *Guastelo v. Michigan C.R. Co.* (Mich.).
- Workers who are on break on or off the employer's premises during the normal workday.

Injuries occurring during rest or eating periods at an authorized place provided by the employer are compensable. Most courts have held that if the meal is taken off premises, resulting injuries are not compensable. But a minority have decided to the contrary, as for example, the courts in *Littlefield v. Pillsbury Co.* (Ohio) (employee returning from break and injured in a motor vehicle accident just outside the entrance to employer's premises) and *Hornyak v. Great Atlantic & Pacific Tea Co.* (N.J.). Jurisdictions are about evenly split on the compensability of injuries sustained during breaks on the employer's premises but away from authorized lunch or recreation areas. In particular fact patterns, findings of compensability have been premised on determinations that an employee was exposed to a special hazard by the nature of employment (e.g., a taxi driver forced to eat in cafeterias, *Relkin v. National Transp. Co. (N.Y.)*).

- Employees who are injured during work as a result of horseplay or quarrels with co-workers.

  These employees are covered by workers' compensation if they did not initiate the activity but were only innocent victims. There is a trend toward liberalization of the general rule if the horseplay is an expected part of the employment (e.g., messenger boys shooting paper clips from rubber bands, *Johnson v. Loew's* (N.Y.)), but a small number of decisions do not appear to recognize claims for *any* injuries resulting from horseplay (e.g., the Georgia case of *Kight v. Liberty Mutual Ins. Co.*).

- Employees who violate work rules and are injured.

  Misconduct of this sort does not render injuries noncompensable unless the rule that is violated is so basic to the job that the worker is removed from the sphere of employment, as in the case of South Carolina police chief who, in violation of work rules, rode in a fire truck and was thereby injured *(Black v. Town of Springfield)*.

Going and Coming

Injuries sustained while traveling between home and a fixed situs of employment are generally not compensable. This general rule is coming under attack, and exceptions are being construed liberally. The rule does not apply to employees who do not have a fixed place of employment. Exceptions to this "going and coming" rule include:

- If the employer provides the transportation, then the injuries sustained by the employee are usually considered to arise out of employment. This exception is by no means universally applied, however. The Arizona appeals court decision in *Rencehausen v. Western Greyhound Lines,* denying compensation under these circumstances, represents the view of the minority.
- If the employee has some duty at home or en route, such that the activity of traveling between work and home becomes an incident of employment.
- If the employee is paid for his or her time or expense in traveling back and forth, then traveling is sometimes considered to be in the course of the employment. Some states have definitely rejected this exception to the going and coming rule, e.g., *Orsinie v. Torrance* (Conn.). The North Carolina Supreme Court in *Hunt v. State* apparently rejected the exception but an appellate decision from that state, *Warren v. Wilmington,* held that the fact that an injured worker was being paid for her travel time was at least a factor in allowing her claim. The shift in attitude of North Carolina's judiciary reflects a general acceptance of this exception across the nation.
- If the employee uses his or her own vehicle in the performance of job duties, then some courts have held that injuries sustained in that vehicle on the way to or from work are compensable. A California appellate decision, *Rhodes v. Workers' Compensation Appeals Board,* explains the rationale for this exception—which appears to be uniformly applied in similar cases: the employees are *required* by their employment to submit to the hazards of private motor travel, which otherwise they would have the option of avoiding.
- If employees are required to take unusual hazards in traveling to or from work, for example, crossing rail-

road tracks, injuries sustained are sometimes said to arise out of employment. This is not a well-recognized exception to the general rule of noncompensability of going and coming injuries and was definitely rejected by the Michigan Supreme Court in *Guastelo v. Michigan C.R. Co.* When invoked by a court to allow a claim, the exception is often limited to claims for injuries sustained in those areas directly under control of the employer (e.g., *Utah Apex Mining Co. v. Industrial Comm'n of Utah (Utah)*).

Injuries Caused by the Worker's Own Fault

Fault of the worker—from simple negligence or carelessness to violations of safety rules, intoxication, or intentional self-infliction—may be implicated in many ways in an accident or injury sustained in the course of employment.

Injuries stemming from horseplay and quarrels among coemployees and violations of regular work rules were discussed previously as giving rise to questions regarding their work-relatedness. These categories of injuries are not included in the present employee-fault discussion because, regardless of whether a particular jurisdiction has special exception from coverage for "employee fault," injuries involving horseplay or employee quarrels always raise the question of whether an injury arose out of employment or was work-related. The present discussion focuses on injuries implicating certain statutory provisions or judicial decisions, which are based on a perceived public policy that some injuries should not be compensable *even though they may be work related* because they were caused at least in part by the fault of the injured worker.

Negligence; Purposeful Self-Infliction. These two extremes of injury categories involving the worker's fault are the easiest to deal with. Injuries that are caused by the worker's negligence are generally compensable (although Wyoming does not allow compensation for injuries "caused totally" by employees' negligence), and those injuries that are purposely self-inflicted are generally never compensable. The middle categories are more troubling. In conflict are two general approaches to the issue, each of which has its own relatively cogent rationale.

The first is that the fault of either the employer or the employee is not really relevant to the compensability of a particular injury. Under this rubric, the question is never who was at fault. Rather, it is simply, was the injury work-related. Hence, purposefully self-inflicted injuries are noncompensable, not because the worker committed a "wrong," but simply because the injury arose out of the worker's intentional act rather than out of employment.

A second approach views workers' compensation as a system designed to replace common-law negligence actions with a comprehensive insurance system. It was never designed to replace other sorts of torts and, therefore, by committing misconduct of a more serious nature such as recklessly or willfully disregarding safety rules, workers remove themselves from the compensation system.

Willful Misconduct. The term that most often is used to preclude recovery in this context is "willful misconduct," a term borrowed from the tort and criminal law fields. Exceptions for coverage or work-related injuries go against the grain of the basic compensability-regardless-of-fault premise of a workers' compensation system. Consequently, this willful misconduct exception has been difficult to apply or define, since the concept of fault has little application or specific meaning in the workers' compensation context. Moreover, the wholesale borrowing of the concept and various definitions from other fields rather begs the question and adds to the confusion.

Consider, for example, an employee who is injured as a result of violating a criminal statute. The Georgia Supreme Court in *Aetna Ins. Co. v. Carroll* applied what it must have thought was a common-sense rule and held that an injury that resulted from the worker's violation of a motor vehicle speed law, a criminal statute, was not compensable. This blanket rule, which apparently was applied in *Aetna,* has found little favor elsewhere and was specifically found to be "unacceptable" to the Superior Court of Delaware in *Carey v. Bryan & Rollins.*

Partly because of such definitional problems and partly because of the liberal construction to be afforded to workers' compensation law, the term "willful misconduct" in workers' compensation cases generally has been strictly construed as requiring premeditation. "Inexcusable ignorance" or bad judgment alone do not rise to this level.

The Virginia Supreme Court, however, in *Mills v. Virginia Electric Co.*, disallowed a claim for an injury that resulted from deliberate disregard of a reasonable safety rule. *Mills* construed such disregard of a safety rule that was designed to prevent the type of injury that actually resulted to be the sort of willful misconduct that renders work-related injuries noncompensable.

Safety Violations as Separate Employer Defense. Some statutes state that injuries resulting from an employee's violation of a safety rule or safety statute will not be compensable. But they provide for the issue to be raised as a separate employer's defense—that is to say, separate from the defense of willful misconduct or the defense that the safety-rule violation removed the worker from the course of employment. This defense is difficult in theory and rarely successful in practice.

It is worth remembering that workers' compensation is designed as general, no-fault insurance coverage for work-related risks. The safety hazards of employment, which include the hazards caused by safety-rule violations of workers and fellow employees, are certainly within any reasonable understanding of the term "risk of employment."

In practice, one appellate court in Georgia, in *Young v. American Ins. Co.*, denied compensation because an employee who was involved in a motor-vehicle accident was driving 100 miles per hour in a 70 mile-per-hour speed zone. Otherwise, few, if any, recent cases have denied recovery to a worker as a penalty for that employee's safety violation. It is better to approach these factual situations as "in the course of and arising out of employment" questions and inquire merely whether the violation was of such a magnitude that the injury was not work-related.

Intoxication. Like injuries arising from the employee's violation of a safety rule, injuries that result from the injured worker's intoxication are not automatically noncompensable unless the state statute so requires. In the absence of a statutory provision, the usual question is whether the intoxication was such that it removed the worker from the course of employment, i.e., whether it constituted an intervening cause for the injury.

MENTAL STRESS CLAIMS

A growing number of jurisdictions are recognizing workers' compensation injury claims for medical conditions that result from workplace stress. As discussed earlier in this chapter, some states still require physical trauma in injury claims. Others continue to require a physical result. But a growing number of cases are accepting claims for medical conditions caused by work-related stress and for mental disabilities that result from working conditions.

Payment under workers' compensation for mental conditions that have resulted from physical disabilities in already recognized claims is a legal commonplace. For instance, in the federal case, *Atlantic Marine, Inc. v. Bruce*, a claim for low-back pain under the Longshore and Harborworkers' Compensation Act gave rise to a compensable "anxiety and depressive reaction," which, in turn, gave rise to a compensable heart attack.

Mental stress that results from shocking specific incidents is often found to be compensable. Thus, a worker's "paranoid schizophrenia" that developed after he witnessed a co-worker in flames was found compensable by a Wisconsin appeals court in *International Harvester v. Labor & Industry Review Comm'n*.

In claims involving allegations of non-specific job stress as the cause of mental conditions, the states continue to be split. Some, like Tennessee by court decision in *Henley v. Roadway Express* and Ohio by statute, continue to require specific or physical trauma. Others, like Connecticut appear to draw no real distinctions between stress-caused disabilities and other work-related problems. See *Kiernan v. Roadway Express*.

Many other states are attempting to draw middle-of-the road approaches to the issue. When an Oregon claimant alleges job-stress as the causative agent of a mental disability, his or her claim must be subjected to an objective test. If the individual's stress is based on a misperception or an overreaction to a work environment, then the mental condition is caused by the worker's misperception rather than by work. See discussion in *(Oregon) State Accident Insurance Fund Corp. v. Griffith.*

Arizona's Supreme Court requires simply that claimants show that job stress is something other than the ordinary stresses of employment to which all workers are subjected. See *Sloss v. Industrial Comm'n.*

For a discussion of mental-stress disabilities as occupational disease claims, see Chapter 3.

PRE-EXISTING MEDICAL CONDITIONS

The uniformly applied rule with regard to workers who suffer from injuries that aggravate or exacerbate already-existing medical conditions is that injuries that aggravate such conditions are fully compensable. This is based on the principle that the employer takes its workers as it finds them with all their medical conditions, weaknesses, and infirmities. If the injury giving rise to the claim was due to the normal progress of the disease and not due to any employment condition, however, it did not arise out of employment and therefore is not compensable.

The distinction between exacerbation and aggravation of a pre-existing condition is significant. An aggravation is a general worsening of an underlying condition and the allowance of a claim for an aggravation of a pre-existing condition is generally regarded as a recognition of the entire condition. An exacerbation, on the other hand, in a one-time "flare-up" of the condition and the recognition of a claim for an exacerbation requires payment only for the duration of the flare-up.

In the absence of a special provision, there is no cost set-off or apportionment for the pre-existing condition, and if a compensable injury results in an aggravation, the worker is entitled to full benefits for the condition. Apportionment of the compensation between the injury and the pre-existing condition also is not proper in the absence of a special statute to that effect.

Alleviation of employer's financial burden for taking on workers who are handicapped or who suffer from medical problems is usually accomplished through the device of the *second-injury fund* (see Chapter 9) or similar program for reimbursing the employer for costs of such claims or spreading the costs over the entire workers' compensation system.

BENEFITS AND ACCRUAL OF RIGHTS

The right to benefits for a workers' compensation injury or accident claim are fixed as of the date the injury or accident was incurred. Generally speaking, subsequent statutory changes in, for example, weekly compensation rates or "substantive" conditions of coverage—including applicable statutes of limitations—have no effect on the claimant's rights and compensation levels. The rule knows a general exception as phrased by the California appeals court in *Industrial Indemnity Co. v. Workers' Compensation Appeals Board:* The law in effect at time of injury or disablement applies, unless there is clear legislative intent to make changes in the law retroactive.

3
Occupational Diseases

The technical definition of the term "occupational disease" (OD) varies among workers' compensation systems and, sometimes, within one system. In some systems the term means a disability that is caused by prolonged exposure at work and is not otherwise distinguished from an injury. In others the term is applied only to specifically listed ailments that are presumptively caused by certain occupations. It has also been suggested that ODs are distinguishable from accidents or injuries because they cannot really be said to be "unexpected," as accidents, by definition, are. (See Chapter 2.)

It is best for most purposes, however, to apply a commonsense definition to the term, that is, to think of occupational diseases as those ailments that are associated with particular industrial trades or processes. Obvious examples include coal miners' pneumoconiosis or "black lung" disease, radiation illness, silicosis, and the asbestos-related diseases notoriously associated with the insulation industry. Not-so-obvious examples would include arthritis caused by repetitive trauma or vibrations associated with some physical labor, mental-stress ailments associated with high-pressure positions, and, perhaps certain cardiovascular problems sometimes said to be connected with the police and firefighting professions.

As noted in Chapter 1, some jurisdictions provide no separate definitional category for occupational diseases. In practice, the distinction between the two categories is becoming more and more vague and less important. The comments by Arthur Larson, an authority in the field of workers' compensation, regarding the distinction between injury and occupational disease are worth bearing in mind:

> The important boundary becomes now, not that separating occupational disease from accident, since compensability lies on both sides of that boundary, but the boundary separating occupational disease from diseases that are neither accidental nor occupational, but common to mankind and not distinctively associated with employment.

This scholar also suggests that what separates occupational diseases from accidents is that the former cannot really be said to be unexpected, since such diseases are recognized as an inherent hazard of employment and are gradual rather than sudden in onset.

Virtually any disease that is caused by an industrial trade or process can be recognized as an occupational disease. In those jurisdictions in which occupational diseases are distinguished from injuries, coverage is provided by statutes that generally recognize occupational diseases or by statutes that list certain "scheduled" ailments as recognized occupational diseases associated with certain trades or industrial processes, or by both. "Scheduled" diseases and "other" diseases are discussed in the next section. In those states that still require physical trauma for injury claims, a claim for a disability caused solely by mental stress can be brought only as an occupational disease.

OCCUPATIONAL DISEASE COVERAGE

Scheduled Diseases

Many states have statutes that list certain ailments as occupational diseases for certain industrial trades or processes. Inclusion in such a schedule "appears to establish a strong presumption that the contraction of that disease by one engaged in the process was attributable to the employment, while the contraction of the same disease in another process would require definite affirmative proof of causal connection."

The statutory provisions for coverage of occupational diseases vary from state to state. Some provide schedules of such diseases, others do not. Those states which have schedules also may include a catch-all provision. The "schedules" of some states contain only one disease listed separately from the general accident or injury provision, while New York's schedule lists 29 diseases, and Ohio's and North Carolina's, 27 each. The diseases most often occurring on schedules include the various pneumoconioses which are associated with exposure to dusts (including coal dust), silicosis from exposure to silica, asbestosis, and radiation illness.

Other Diseases

Under a general or "catch-all" provision, essentially effective in all U.S. jurisdictions, an occupational disease is compensable if it is caused by employment. Many states have a provision stating that such diseases are compensable if they are "peculiar to an industrial trade or process." This means that the employment exposes workers to a higher risk of contracting the disease than that to which the general public is exposed. The Ohio Supreme Court addressed this definition in *Ohio Bell Telephone Co. v. Krise,* in which it allowed a claim for histoplasmosis incurred by a telephone lineman's exposure to pigeon droppings. The case contains a good and generally applicable discussion of the phrase "peculiar to an industrial trade or process."

As a corollary to the broadness of this phrase or definition, no exhaustive list of pertinent diseases or medical problems is practical. Following are observations on coverage of some specific ailments or conditions:

- *Hernias* are often compensable and, in those jurisdictions that differentiate injuries from occupational diseases, they are usually classified as injuries. Like many states, Florida's law provides specific limitations on length of compensation for hernia victims *(Plant City Steel v. Grace)*, and on conditions for coverage of this condition *(Metropolitan Dade County Bd. of Comm'r v. Wyche)*. Mississippi's provision is similar. *(Bechtel Constr. Co. v. Bartlett)*.

- *Hearing loss allegedly from noisy environments* is usually so gradual and its etiology so difficult to ascertain that several states have set out special restrictions on compensability.

  A majority of states treat hearing loss as an occupational disease rather than an injury, but the Pennsylvania Supreme Court in *Hinkle v. H.J. Heinz Co.* treated it as an injury on a "repeated trauma" basis. Some states have set up separate statutory provisions for hearing loss, the most impressive of which is New York's, which provides a separate waiting period, definition of disablement, apportionment of liability among employers, and minimum exposure guideline. The provision in Wisconsin's "Occupational Deafness" statute, that no compensation is payable for temporary total or temporary partial disability resulting from occupational deafness, is not unusual. Ohio provides for no permanent-partial disability awards for less-than-total loss of hearing in one ear.
- *Allergies* are subject to varying treatment among the states according to particular circumstances; however, some principles seem fairly well established. The mere fact that an individual has an allergy before beginning employment does not render subsequent manifestations of the allergic condition noncompensable. Generally speaking, if work occasions an exposure to an irritant to which the worker is already allergic, that specific incident is a compensable injury but the underlying condition is not. On the other hand, an individual who develops a sensitivity to an irritant because of work exposure will probably have a compensable occupational disease claim in most U.S. jurisdictions. Moreover, it appears that allergies are compensable if employment exposes a worker to an irritant to which he is unknowingly allergic. In *Webb v. New Mexico Publishing Co.* (N.M.) such an allergy claim was allowed, but as an injury, not as an occupational disease.

  Many states provide in their statutes for "contact dermatitis," a condition resulting from exposure to chemical irritants. Two states have rejected allergic reactions as occupational diseases, *Kelly-Springfield Tire Co. v. Roland* (Md.); *Sanford v. Valier-Spies Milling Co.* (Mo.).

- *Mental disabilities or stress-caused illnesses* present a special problem. As a general rule, psychiatric conditions that are proved to be the result of an already allowed injury or occupational disease are compensable as part of the underlying claim. The psychiatric condition is allowed as a "flow-through" disability, much like traumatic arthritis is commonly allowed as a "flow-through" in injury claims initially allowed for fractures. Although special procedures—such as the claimant's completing and filing of an affidavit regarding psychiatric history—may sometimes be required, there is no legal problem with allowance of such conditions *as part of an already allowed claim*.

A legal problem sometimes arises when mental stress or emotional trauma is the *only* cause of the disability. In states which still require some sort of physical trauma or sudden occurrence in injury claims, emotional trauma obviously cannot form such a predicate, since even when emotionally traumatic instances are sudden, they are, by definition, not physically traumatic. In such jurisdictions, claimants must attempt to prove that their emotionally induced disabilities are occupational diseases. They therefore must establish that their employment was of such a nature as to expose them in a "peculiar" way to such emotional distress. Not surprisingly, allowances of claims for mental distress as occupational diseases have not fared well for claimants. *Voss v. Prudential Ins. Co.* (N.J.) and *Szymanski v. Halle's* (Ohio) have refused to recognize mental-distress disabilities as injuries, while *Transportation Ins. Co. v. Maksyn* (Tex.) refused to recognize such disability as an occupational disease.

However, in those jurisdictions that provide no legal impediment to claims for mental distress, such claims have often been allowed as injuries when the work-related incidents giving rise to the disability were particularly stressful.

Some authorities have noted a trend toward allowance of mental-distress claims, whether as an injury or as an occupational disease: *Carter v. General Motors Corp.* (Mich.). See also Justice Sweeney's dissent in *Szymanski v. Halle's* (Ohio).

WORK-RELATEDNESS

As noted in the discussion of injuries in Chapter 2, a premise for allowance of any workers' compensation claim is that the disabled worker has established the work-relatedness of the disability. For injuries, work-relatedness is established by a showing that the injury was sustained "in the course of and arising out of employment."

Causal connection between employment and an occupational disease is determined in accordance with the literal terms of the statutes pertaining to scheduled diseases or the language that nonscheduled diseases must be "peculiar to an industrial trade or process."

As noted in the previous discussion of scheduled diseases, inclusion of a disease on a statutory schedule creates a strong presumption that the disease is associated with an industry or a trade. While a medical diagnosis is still required in such cases, the work-relatedness of the condition is, at least rebuttably, a given.

On the other hand, an individual who alleges contraction of a nonscheduled occupational disease is required to establish that the condition is "peculiar to an industrial trade or process." This generally means proof—including medical proof—that the employment exposed the worker to the risk of contracting the condition in a way that members of the public generally are not exposed.

PRE-EXISTING CONDITIONS

In those jurisdictions that treat occupational diseases differently from injuries, pre-existing conditions are sometimes also treated differently. In some states, aggravation of a pre-existing condition may not be recognized as an occupational disease. Although some courts now reject the rule that aggravation of a pre-existing condition is noncompensable as an occupational disease, *Czepial v. Krohne Roofing Co.* (Fla.), the rule of noncompensability has been recently re-affirmed by the Ohio Supreme Court, *Miller v. Ohio ex rel. Mead.* (These divergent results have been reached despite the similar statutory schemes of Ohio and Florida.) A few states, such as Illinois, have statutes which specifically allow for aggravation of pre-existing diseases under the occupational disease statute.

The rationale precluding occupational disease coverage for pre-existing conditions is that, if a disease must be "contracted in the course of employment" and "peculiar to an industrial trade or process," then medical conditions that pre-exist employment cannot form the basis of an occupational disease claim.

This rule of noncompensability does not apply, however, if the pre-existing condition was itself occupational in origin. And it does not mean that a disease occasioned by the conditions of work operating on a particularly susceptible individual is not compensable. Such individuals are entitled to compensation even though the method of allocation of the claim may place an unfair or disproportionate burden on the employer of last injurious exposure.

APPORTIONMENT AND ALLOCATION OF COSTS OF OCCUPATIONAL DISEASE CLAIMS

Kansas, like some other states, has a statutory provision for apportioning the cost of an occupational disease claim. The usual method requires the workers' compensation administrative body to make a determination that a certain percentage of the disease was caused by employment and to assess only that percentage of the costs of the disease to the claim. *Fuentes v. Workers' Compensation Appeals Board* (Cal.) and *Riverside of Marks v. Russell* (Miss.) contain good discussions of apportionment principles.

Statutes in 10 states and the District of Columbia specifically provide for the allocations of costs of an occupational disease claim to the last employer of injurious exposure. The unfairness of this rule in particular instances is alleviated somewhat by the mechanism of the *second-injury fund* (See Chapter 9) and by statutes providing for apportionment of costs. It is fairly well established, however, that in the absence of such provisions, deficiencies in the methods of allocating the costs of a claim will not defeat a claimant's rights to compensation.

SPECIAL CONDITIONS OF COVERAGE (TIME LIMITATIONS)

Special restrictive statutes, primarily statutes of limitations, apply in the occupational disease schemes of many states. Although the modern trend has been toward elimination of such restrictions, they remain at least in some modified form in the laws of many jurisdictions. The U.S. Chamber of Commerce Chart, "Coverage of Occupational Diseases," Appendix B, breaks down the various restrictions, jurisdiction-by-jurisdiction. These restrictions most commonly apply in claims for dust-caused diseases of the respiratory tract.

- *Minimal exposure rules* require that the claimant have been working in the injurious environment for a minimum period of time. The statutes often have required that the minimum exposure occur "in this state" for a minimum period.
- *Onset-of-disability rules* require that disability or death have ensued within a certain period of time from the date of the claimant's last injurious exposure. Sometimes the rule is stated conversely, that is, a presumption of causation will attach if death or disability begin within the time period. The rule is often modified or eliminated in death claims if, before death, the worker became totally disabled within the ascribed time period.
- *Rules requiring injurious exposure after a certain date* or injurious exposure "in this state" after a certain date are self-explanatory. They are still in force in many states as a vestige of minimal exposure rules. Often the dates specified are so old that the statutes are obsolete.
- *Medical examinations* are required under many statutes prior to allowance of occupational disease claims. Often the law requires the state agency to refer the claimant

to an independent specialist or to a medical board for an examination before allowing a claim. The opinions of such medical specialists are often only advisory.

Larson's comments on these exclusionary rules reflects the general attitude of courts: "The arbitrariness of these statutes and their exceptions has produced all kinds of senseless discriminations." All of these rules except for the medical examination requirement have been severely criticized and, over the years, have been fading away.

BENEFITS

Benefits for occupational disease claims are usually the same as benefits for injury claims, but some states provide limitations on partial disability for certain occupational diseases and, as noted, some states provide for only an apportioned percentage of the costs of a disease if there is a pre-existing condition. The variety of provisions is shown by the following examples: Alabama and Tennessee provide the same compensation for total disability or death from coal miners' pneumoconiosis as is provided by Federal Black Lung Act. Arkansas provides no partial-disability compensation in asbestosis and silicosis claims if the partial disability is less than 33 and one-third percent. Idaho and South Dakota provide no partial-disability compensation for silicosis. Montana precludes partial-disability compensation for any occupational disease. Ohio precludes partial-disability compensation for dust-caused diseases of the respiratory tract. Pennsylvania provides limitations of compensation for silicosis and asbestosis claims.

Several jurisdictions provide special additional or substitute benefits for victims of occupational diseases, the most common of which is the *change of occupation* award. These awards are discussed in Chapter 5.

As with injury or accident claimants, an individual's rights to benefits and compensation for occupational disease or injury are fixed as of the date of inception of the claim. However, since in these cases, there is no particular "date of injury," and the inception of the disease is often a gradual and indefinite process, the date of inception of an occupational disease poses special problems.

The usual method of ascertaining the date is by taking the date of "disability" or "disablement." This usually means the last date the claimant worked or the date on which the claimant was forced to change occupations. Sometimes the date of the diagnosis is considered the determining date and generally is taken to be the date that the claimant is informed by a licensed physician of the nature, extent, and probable occupational nature of the medical condition. In some jurisdictions, the "date of disability" is a grace period that extends the limitations period but presumably does not alter the date of inception of the disease, i.e., the date by which the claimant's rights are fixed.

See U.S. Chamber of Commerce Charts, "Coverage of Occupational Diseases," and "Income Benefits for Total Disability," Appendices B and C, for summaries of state provisions.

4
DEATH CLAIMS

Deaths that occur in the course of and arising out of employment or that are caused by compensable injuries or occupational diseases are compensable as death claims in all jurisdictions. The purpose of death benefits is twofold: to provide a substitute for the financial support that the deceased had been providing to dependents and to pay for burial and miscellaneous death expenses.

The U.S. Chamber of Commerce Chart, "Fatalities—Income Benefits for Spouse & Children," reproduced as Appendix D, contains a jurisdiction-by-jurisdiction listing of death benefits.

WORK-RELATEDNESS OF DEATH

The work-relatedness of a death is established by evidence—usually medical proof—that the death was caused by a compensable injury or an occupational disease. This does not mean, however, that the decedent must have had an allowed *claim* during his or her lifetime in order for the surviving dependents to maintain a separate death claim. Their claim is separate and independent from any injury or occupational disease claim that the decedent may have had while he or she was alive. Therefore, the fact that the decedent may have settled a claim for compensation or may not have brought a claim or even that the state agency disallowed a claim during the lifetime of a worker does not bar the survivors' claims for death benefits.

From these premises follows the general rule that employees have no power to release the death claims of their survivors.

Although findings in a claim filed by an employee generally do not have *res judicata* or issue-preclusive effect in a death claim brought by the employee's survivors, as a matter of practice—and in some states, as a matter of law—findings that the injury suffered by an employee *was* compensable amount in a real-world way to controlling findings in a subsequent death claim. The Rhode Island Supreme Court, for example, in *Card v. Lloyd Mfg. Co.*, held that a finding that the deceased's injury arose out of and in the course of his employment was *res judicata* as to a claim filed by the decedent's widow. Thus, the practice regarding issue preclusion may be said to work harder against employers than it does against dependent-claimants.

BENEFITS PAYABLE FOR DEATH CLAIMS

Death benefits in workers' compensation claims include funeral or burial expenses and support for the dependent survivors of the deceased employee.

Weekly benefits for the survivors usually are set at rates that are comparable to benefits for weekly total disability benefits. Generally, the rate is fixed by the rate in effect at time of the employee's *death*, not the date of the employee's injury. This follows from the premise that the survivor's claim for death benefits is independent of any underlying claim of the decedent. *State Compensation Fund v. Stanke*, an Arizona appellate decision, is an example of the minority position—based on a specific state statute—that law in effect at time of injury controls.

Many states provide that unpaid compensation that was accrued in the decedent's lifetime is payable to a surviving spouse after the death of the employee. Some states permit this award to the spouse only if the employee died from a non-work-related cause, a requirement of dubious validity based on the theory that to award both could result in a windfall. Provisions in Ohio's statutes that conditioned a surviving spouse's receipt of accrued compensation upon a showing that the death was not work-related were struck down as violative of equal protection in *Nyitray v. Indus. Comm'n of Ohio* and *LaCavera v. Cleveland Electric Illuminating Co.*

DEPENDENTS OF THE DECEASED EMPLOYEE

Statutes ordinarily define with some particularity the classes of individuals who are entitled to receive death benefits as dependents. The classifications vary widely but as a general matter they may be broken down into three groups: those individuals who are presumed to be dependent on the decedent at the time of death, those who must establish that they were dependent, and those who are not permitted to receive benefits even though they may have been dependent.

Presumed Dependent

This classification includes a spouse who was living with the deceased at the time of death. The spouse is usually required to supply proof of a valid marriage to support the claim. Ex-spouses generally are not entitled to dependency benefits. In states that recognize common-law marriages, a common-law spouse must provide proof of such a marriage—the usual burden for which is "clear and convincing evidence." Once common-law status is established, such spouses are entitled to the same presumption that attaches for individuals who went through a ceremonial marriage.

Surviving children who are minors or who are attending full-time school are also usually presumed to be dependents. "Children" usually includes legitimate children, adopted children, and legitimized children born out of wedlock. A workers' compensation statute that discriminated against illegitimate children was held by the United States Supreme Court in *Weber v. Aetna Casualty & Surety Co.* to be an unconstitutional denial of equal protection of laws.

Many states also provide the presumption of dependency for parents who were living with the deceased worker at the time of death. As discussed below, the parents also are generally among those who are permitted to prove dependency.

While as a technical matter survivors of a deceased worker

who are within one of the above-mentioned classes must be actually dependent upon the worker at the time of death in order to qualify for benefits, the presumption of dependency for such individuals appears to be a strong one, even though it is technically rebuttable.

Permitted Dependent

This group generally includes members of the family who were living with the decedent at the time of death. Many states list those classes of kin—parents, siblings, grandparents, grandchildren, for example—who are permitted to establish that they were dependents. Certain statutes permit other individuals who were members of the deceased's "family" or "household" to prove that they were dependent on the deceased at the time of death.

Circumstances pertaining to dependency matters vary so widely that only the most general observations regarding the issue can be meaningful in the present context. Liberal construction of the statutes pertaining to dependency issues frequently guides courts in resolving the difficult factual questions. Thus, a dependent often is described as one who looked to or relied on the deceased for support and maintenance. This does not mean that the individual absolutely depended on the deceased for the necessities of life but that the survivor relied on contributions of the worker as means of support and maintenance in accordance with social position and accustomed mode of life. *Farnsworth v. Indus. Comm'n* contains a good discussion by the Supreme Court of Utah of dependency issues.

Some states require the claimant to establish that the deceased worker owed him or her a legal obligation of support, but ordinarily such a showing is not prerequisite to establishing dependency. It is necessary, however, that the support or contributions had been made directly to the putative dependent or for such individual's benefit.

Individuals Who Are Not Entitled to Survivor's Benefits

Regardless of whether individuals can establish that they were in fact dependent on the deceased at the time of death, most states exclude everyone not mentioned in the classes of individuals which are listed in the statutes. Some statutes require that those entitled to benefits merely be members of the deceased's "household" or "family," terms that are certainly subject to varying interpretations. But absent such general terms, the rule is clear that any individual not enumerated in the applicable statute may not recover survivor's benefits. While, of course, non-relatives may have been dependents of a deceased worker at the time of death, those individuals who do not come within one of the enumerated classes are not entitled to dependency benefits.

Partial Dependency

The issue of dependency is further complicated by provision in the laws of many jurisdictions that a determination must also be made as to whether the survivor-claimant was *wholly* or *partially* dependent. Generally, the presumption of dependency for surviving spouses and minor children includes a presumption of *total* dependency—a presumption that, as has been noted, is rebuttable but fairly strong. Otherwise, whether dependency exists and is total or partial is a matter of fact and depends on many circumstances. Indicia include the survivor's own income, whether the survivor received support from other sources, and the extent to which the survivor actually relied on the deceased for maintenance.

WORK-RELATEDNESS OF SUICIDE

As has been noted, many statutes provide that injury or death that was purposely self-inflicted is not compensable. Even in the absence of such statutes, purposely self-inflicted injuries ordinarily would not be compensable, since they were not occasioned "in the course of and arising out of employment." (See Chapter 2.) Such rules are not much help in analyzing cases in which individuals become severely depressed or maladjusted as a result of work-related accidents or diseases and take their own lives. As a practical matter, when claims for survivors' benefits are brought by the dependents of suicide victims, the issue is almost never whether the death comes within the statutory or judicially made exception for compensability for injuries that were *purposely* self-inflicted. Rather, the question is whether the injury or disease and its sequellae caused such an emotional or mental illness that either the worker could not entertain a fixed purpose to commit suicide, or he or she was under an irresistible impulse to commit suicide. The evidentiary and burden-of-proof problems in suicide cases are well addressed in the Georgia appellate decision of *McDonald v. Atlantic Steel Corp.*

Wilder v. Russell Library Co., a Connecticut Supreme Court decision, is an example of allowance of a suicide-death claim in a jurisdiction that does not require a showing of an "accident" as a condition of compensability of injuries. The Minnesota Supreme Court in *Schwartz v. Talmo* denied a survivor's claim on the basis of a statute that precluded recovery for suicide.

5

Compensation and Benefits

THE CONCEPT OF DISABILITY AND DISABILITY COMPENSATION

Disability

This term in the workers' compensation context generally means a loss of physical or mental function that adversely affects an individual's ability to earn a living or that results in medical treatment. The "loss of physical or mental function" component of that definition is known as medical impairment, which is, strictly speaking, a medical question, even where it is not expressly recognized as such. Determinations of disability, in contrast, are made by state agencies or other adjudicatory bodies, even where the opinions of medical and other experts on the question are admitted.

It follows that, in all jurisdictions, a physician may render an opinion admissible in workers' compensation proceedings on the degree of impairment that a claimant has suffered as a result of an injury or occupational disease. Generally, the adjudicating agency will be bound by medical evidence on the question of impairment. Thus, if a claimant's physician opines that an injury has resulted in a 20 percent permanent impairment, the insurer's physician is of the same opinion, and no other medical evidence contradicts this finding, then as a general rule the agency must find that the claimant suffers a 20 percent impairment as a result of the injury. But in most states it would not necessarily follow that the agency must then grant the claimant a 20 percent disability award. It must still determine the claimant's disability, that is, the effect of the claimant's impairment on his or her ability to earn a living. Factors other than medical impairment that enter into determinations of disability include the claimant's regular employment, age, education, training, and the demand for the claimant's skills in the geographical area.

In many jurisdictions, physicians' opinions on extent of the claimant's disability are probative, although in some places their opinions are strictly limited to the issue of extent of medical impairment. An example of admissibility of a medical expert's opinion on the "ultimate question" of claimant's disability rather than on the limited question of impairment is contained in a decision from the U.S. Court of Appeals for the Seventh Circuit, *Allen v. Weinberger*. The *Allen* court was required to go through some intellectual gymnastics because of strict requirements regarding admissibility of opinions on "ultimate" questions. The court construed the opinion "as an indicator of how severe the patient's impairment was at the time of the examination." In most jurisdictions, the exercise in *Allen* would not be necessary as physicians' opinions on the ultimate question are probative. However, in *International Coal & Mining Co. v. Industrial Comm'n*, an old case from the Illinois Supreme Court representing the minority view, the court refused even to admit a physician's opinion on the "ultimate question."

The American Medical Association's *Guides to the Evaluation of Permanent Impairment* is generally recognized as authoritative, and some statutes, for example, Nevada's, specifically refer to it.

Disability Compensation

Most kinds of compensation available in workers' compensation systems are attempts to compensate for loss of either earnings or earning capacity and are usually paid or accrued weekly. The basis for an award of compensation is the worker's earnings at the time of injury or death, and the amount is generally not governed by the nature or location of the injury or the manner of inception of the disease. It is only the extent of the disability or, on occasion, impairment, that is the measure of the compensation awarded.

The terms "compensation" and "benefits" are sometimes used interchangeably but for the sake of clarity the connotative distinctions between them are worth bearing in mind. "Benefits" is the generic term that includes compensation payable directly to claimants in the form of cash benefits and any other payment made under the claim such as amounts for medical care, rehabilitation services, travel expenses, attorney fees, and funeral payments.

While "compensation" is sometimes used as a synonym for "benefits," it is better to limit its meaning to those "cash" benefits that are payable directly to claimants for permanent total disability, temporary total disability, permanent partial disability, temporary partial disability, and dependent survivors' benefits in death claims.

The various kinds of compensation for disability resulting from workers' compensation injuries or diseases have different purposes. Some are straightforward substitutes for wages; others are for loss of earning capacity (a different concept); some are reimbursement for medical impairment or for loss of physical or mental function; and one—death benefits—is designed as a substitute for lost financial support from the killed worker.

Compensation for disability is calculated on the basis of the worker's weekly wage at the time of injury or death. In a typical jurisdiction, a claimant could get 66⅔ percent of his or her average weekly wage but not more than an amount equal to the statewide average weekly wage during periods of total disability. A few states still have a ceiling on the total accrued benefits or on accrued awards of certain types of compensation.

While certain kinds of awards—most notably scheduled losses, facial disfigurement, and unscheduled permanent-partial disability—may be efforts to compensate an injured worker for medical impairment, these are not "make whole" remedies of the sort contemplated in contract or tort law. Rather they are simply statutory awards designed to grant *some* recognition for the loss of physical or mental functioning occasioned by a claimant's work.

Extent of Disability

Extent of disability has two dimensions: duration and degree. Duration of disability centers on whether the disability is permanent or temporary; degree centers on whether it is partial or total. From this deceptively simple paradigm it might be assumed that there are four permutations and that a straightforward analysis would therefore deal with permanent total disability, temporary total disability, permanent partial disability, and temporary partial disability.

But the various temporary and/or partial disabilities are variously defined and can often result in differing kinds of compensation. Moreover, the two-dimensional paradigm does not take into account rehabilitation benefits and certain so-called impairment awards.

PERMANENT TOTAL DISABILITY

Permanent total disability has a fairly standard definition and is applied with some uniformity across the United States. Claimants who establish that an allowed injury or occupational disease has rendered them unable to engage in substantially remunerative employment are entitled to permanent total disability benefits.

In many jurisdictions claimants who suffer some severe, statutorily defined type of injury or impairment—total blindness of both eyes or loss of two limbs, for example—are presumed to be permanently and totally disabled. Often this presumption is irrebuttable and such claimants are entitled to continued benefits even if they obtain employment after they have been declared permanently and totally disabled.

Otherwise, the general rule is that permanent total disability compensation continues until the occurrence of one of the following events:

- the claimant returns to substantially remunerative employment;
- the claimant dies;
- (where applicable) the claimant exhausts the maximum dollar limit set by statute.

The burden of proving entitlement to permanent total disability benefits is on the claimant, unless the claimant is in one of the presumed-disabled categories described above. Proof generally involves medical and other evidence that takes into account the claimant's age, education, training, sex, regular employment, and likelihood of rehabilitation.

In some states permanent total disability is not lawfully available to claimants who have not availed themselves of rehabilitation services offered by the state, the insurer, or the employer. (See below.) Many workers' compensation agencies refer all applicants for permanent total disability benefits—or at least all applicants under a certain age—to the state rehabilitation agency before making any determination on the issue. Utah, for example, requires claimants who are tentatively found to be permanently and totally disabled to be referred to rehabilitation.

The U.S. Chamber of Commerce Chart, "Income Benefits for Total Disability," Appendix C, contains a breakdown of benefits available in the various states and U.S. jurisdictions.

Substantially remunerative employment is a chameleon of a term that changes its color and shadings according to the immediate background of the facts of each claim. A 50-year-old coal miner with an eighth-grade education and 25 years at the same job may be completely removed from substantially remunerative employment by a back injury that has resulted in a permanent medical impairment of only 20 percent. The issue of permanent and total disability in such cases might be addressed by determining, first that the worker is certainly removed from his regular employment involving heavy manual labor, and second, that it is unlikely he could be retrained or could ever perform any other type of work. Similarly, a hand injury to a highly skilled surgeon or to a pianist could conceivably result in such a high degree of disability as to remove such individuals from an ability to engage in substantially remunerative employment.

By the same token, however, a severe back impairment suffered by, for example, an accountant or a lawyer, might have a relatively minor effect on long-term ability to earn a living. Such individuals might have a more difficult time establishing that they are permanently and totally disabled.

From this discussion three things should become apparent. First, and most obviously, permanent total disability is not the same as permanent and total medical impairment. Total medical impairment is generally thought of as complete inability to perform any of the activities of daily living and "100 percent impairment" is sometimes said to be the equivalent of a permanent comatose state or, perhaps, permanent quadriplegia. (Although it has been suggested that since quadriplegics can still speak and move their face they retain some physical functioning and, therefore, are not totally medically impaired!)

Second, while claimants have the burden of proving that they are permanently and totally disabled, they are not required to prove with absolute certainty that they will never engage in remunerative employment. Their burden is to establish that they have been removed from employment and that it is more probable than not that their medical condition will continue indefinitely and will remove them from employment for the foreseeable future.

Finally, the purpose of permanent and total disability is to compensate the injured worker for loss of *earning capacity*, not to compensate for loss of actual wages. It is an award for *prospective* loss, even though it is usually measured by the amount of wages the worker was earning at the time of injury, accident, or inception of occupational disease.

TEMPORARY TOTAL DISABILITY

This is the most commonly awarded disability compensation under workers' compensation. It is payable during the acute post-injury phase of disability, while the claimant is in the hospital or recuperating from an injury, and so long as the injury keeps the claimant who has an expectation of returning to the job or to the job market from work.

The threshold issue in determinations of temporary total disability is whether the claimant can return to regular employment. In some states, this threshold determination is virtually an irrebuttable presumption until a determination is made as to whether the claimant's injury has become permanent. The Ohio Supreme Court, for example, in *Horne v. Great Lakes Constr. Co.*, held that, at least until a condition is determined to have become permanent, inability to return to the former employment mandates payment of temporary total disability.

Temporary total disability is the basic wage-substitute benefit and its purpose is to compensate a worker for loss of wages during recovery. It is generally measured as a percentage—usually 66⅔ percent—of the worker's full or average weekly wage up to a statutory maximum rate and, in some places, up to a statutory accrued amount.

There is a *waiting period* in most states for temporary total disability, which means that there are no benefits payable for the initial short period of time—usually from one to two weeks—following the disability, unless disability continues for a specified period of time—usually two to three weeks.

TEMPORARY PARTIAL DISABILITY

"Temporary partial disability" is more a generic phrase than it is a legal term, more descriptive than it is definable. Although it occurs as a specific category of compensation in the laws of many states, it often is nothing more than a category of wage-loss or impairment-in-earnings compensation. The District of Columbia statutory scheme, for instance, contains "wage loss" and "temporary partial disability" compensation categories, both of which are calculated in largely the same way, "temporary partial" being paid prior to a claimant's reaching maximum medical improvement, and "wage loss" being paid in certain types of claims afterwards.

It is best for present purposes to treat temporary partial disability compensation as a "catch-all" name for various types of compensation that are payable to claimants who can engage in some remunerative employment but whose injuries have had a negative effect on their earnings, earning capacity, or employability.

Impairment In Earning Capacity

Many states provide for impairment in earning capacity as a form of partial disability compensation. Compensation for impairments in earnings made under the rubric of either permanent partial disability or temporary partial disability are distinguishable both from temporary total disability, which is designed as a substitute for actual loss of wages and is generally paid at a higher weekly rate, and from permanent total disability benefits, which, though designed to compensate workers for loss of earning capacity, is the maximum benefit available under workers' compensation.

Although the usual way to compute impairments in earning capacity is to calculate the difference or a percentage of the difference between the weekly wages earned at the time of disability and the weekly wages earned afterwards, the general rule is that partial disability compensation for impairment in earning capacity has no inherent connection to actual loss of earnings. Although reduction in a claimant's weekly earnings may be evidence—at times presumptive evidence—of impairment in earning capacity, it generally is not conclusive.

Partial disability compensation for impairment in earning capacity has been limited to the actual amount of loss of weekly earnings in *Federico's Case* (Mass.) and *Standard Surety & Casualty Co. v. Sloan* (Tenn.). In such states, the award is in reality a true wage-impairment award rather than an award for impairment in earning capacity.

Factors that may indicate that a claimant's actual loss in weekly wages is not reflective of compensable impairment in earning capacity include wage loss due to worker's fault subsequent to injury, to illness not connected to injury, to general business depression, or to an inability to obtain employment for reasons not the result of the injury or occupational disease.

Unless the statutory scheme is so worded that such an interpretation is not possible, the mere fact that a claimant's weekly earnings may be equal to or even greater than the average weekly wage at the time of the injury or occupational disease does not necessarily mean that there is no compensable wage impairment, since the claimant's capacity to earn may still have diminished. For example, an electrician was held entitled to an impairment in earning capacity award after sustaining fractures to the left wrist and pelvis, even though he had returned to his regular employment and and was receiving higher wages than his average weekly wage before the injury. *Guzman v. Surge Electric* (Fla.).

Wage Loss

In many jurisdictions, temporary partial disability is available for wage loss or for loss of actual earnings. Such compensation is distinguishable from impairment-in-earning-capacity awards in that it compensates for only the actual amount of lost wages. It does not purport to compensate for loss of earning "capacity," and usually pays only a percentage of the difference between pre-injury weekly earnings and post-injury weekly earnings.

In many jurisdictions, wage-loss is one of several types of "temporary partial" compensation. In some places, such as the District of Columbia, it is technically not payable until after a claimant has achieved "maximum medical impairment" and, thus, is really a form of "permanent partial disability."

Change of Occupations

Montana, North Carolina, Ohio, and Utah provide that workers who have suffered from occupational diseases are eligible for "change of occupation awards," which are fixed weekly benefits for certain periods of time or fixed lump sums, if the workers would continue to suffer from injurious exposure at their former place of employment.

In order to qualify for these awards, claimants usually must establish the following:

- that they suffer from an occupational disease;

- that it is medically recommended that they change their occupations to reduce or eliminate further injurious exposure;
- that they actually change their occupations.

Claimants who leave positions that subjected them to injurious exposure are generally deemed to have "changed" occupations for purposes of establishing the third element of eligibility for change of occupation awards, even if they do not obtain another job. See *Ferris v. Ohio Indus. Comm'n* (Ohio).

REHABILITATION

Recognizing that the rehabilitation of injured workers benefits everyone in and around the field of workers' compensation, all but two states—Indiana and South Carolina—have made some effort to incorporate rehabilitation into their workers' compensation systems. These efforts vary widely in form and effect. Usual provisions include an allowance for maintenance and payment by employer, insurer, or special rehabilitation fund for physical and vocational rehabilitation. There is usually a time limit on the length of a claimant's rehabilitation program, typically anywhere from a renewable six-month term to two years.

The maintenance allowance might be as little as board, lodging, and travel, or as much as weekly compensation equivalent to temporary total disability. Rehabilitation in Ohio covers costs for treatment of non-occupational medical conditions that inhibit a claimant's return to work. The costs of relocation are sometimes paid under the rehabilitation program.

In some states continued payment of compensation is conditioned upon a claimant's entering or attempting rehabilitation. In others, applicants for permanent total disability are routinely referred for rehabilitation review to determine whether they are candidates for such services. Usually claimants who are over a specified age—40 or 45—are not reviewed under this procedure.

The prime purpose of rehabilitation is to return the injured worker to the labor market. Another purpose is to limit an employer's or insurer's costs. Thus, compensation is often payable until the claimant can return to the labor market or until it is determined that he or she has failed to co-operate with vocational rehabilitation.

See U.S. Chamber of Commerce Chart, "Rehabilitation of Disabled Workers," Appendix F, for a breakdown of the various states and U.S. jurisdictions.

COMPENSATION FOR MEDICAL IMPAIRMENT PERMANENT PARTIAL DISABILITY

Most workers' compensation systems now make some effort to compensate injured workers for permanent medical impairment or loss of physical or mental functioning that results from an allowed occupational disease or injury. These awards, commonly called permanent partial disability awards, are usually paid irrespective of any actual or prospective loss of wages and are divided into so-called scheduled awards, usually for loss of limb, eyesight, hearing, or for other defined categories of impairments, and non-scheduled permanent partial disability or non-scheduled permanent partial impairment awards.

One reason for establishing these awards was to give injured workers some incentive to return to work; another reason was simply to give workers some quasi-damage award for the physical impairment endured. For both reasons, permanent partial disability awards are usually not affected by the amount of the claimant's post-injury wages. And, although these awards can be quite sizable, they seldom approach the levels awarded in negligence actions by juries for similar injuries.

Objection to these awards is sometimes made on the ground that they betray the basic premises of workers' compensation by taxing the system with costs that appear to lack economic effect. But another more fundamental premise of workers' compensation—that industry should bear the costs of the personal injuries that it causes—is fully consistent with permanent partial disability awards. Moreover, at least in some jurisdictions, the award is viewed as another way for the system to compensate for those sorts of economic effects that, though real, are difficult to quantify.

Non-Scheduled Awards

States that provide for non-scheduled permanent partial disability awards are split on the manner of measuring such awards. Some states base the calculation of permanent partial disability awards strictly upon medical impairments. Nevada uses this approach; it mandates that permanent partial disability awards be based on American Medical Association permanent impairment guidelines.

Other states take a much more liberal view of these awards and require the workers' compensation agencies to make a sort of *ad hoc* determination of the permanent effects that particular medical impairments have upon an individual's ability to earn a living in the job market. Kansas typifies this approach and statutorily defines "extent of (permanent partial) disability" as "the extent, expressed as a percentage, to which the ability of the worker to engage in work of the same type character that was being performed at the time of the injury has been reduced."

Still other states appear to fall somewhere in between and require a determination based upon the effects that this type of injury would have on the average person's ability to earn a living. The Kentucky statute bases permanent partial disability on the percentage of "occupational disability."

In the first type of state, a finding that an individual with an allowed claim for injury to the right hand has, say, 10 percent medical impairment would require an award of 10 percent permanent-partial disability (actually medical impairment) regardless of any other factor.

In the second type of state, such questions as whether the claimant was right-handed, whether his employment required much use of his right hand, the possible effects of the injury on retaining or obtaining employment in the future, and the claimant's age, training, and education could be considered in making adjustments to the amount of compensation awarded.

In the third type of state, a determination would be made as to the amount of permanent disability that this injury would generally be expected to cause to an individual. Inasmuch as medical impairment does not really reflect the actual disability, in the sense that claimants need not establish that they are 100 percent medically impaired in order to establish eligibility for permanent total disability, the state agency may make a reasonable estimate.

Each approach has its advantages and disadvantages. The first has clarity and ease of administration but sacrifices the ability to make adjustments to render fair decisions in particular cases.

The second offers flexibility and the potential for more fairness to individuals but also considerably more room for arbitrariness and abuse. The third approach recognizes that medical impairment really should be translated into disability awards in workers' compensation law, which is designed specifically to compensate for loss of either earnings or earning potential, but offers only the vaguest standards by which to make such determinations.

No effort will be made here to assess any further the relative merits of these various views on permanent partial awards. But employers, employees, and insurers alike should be aware of them and approach the issue accordingly.

Scheduled Awards

Scheduled awards, as previously noted, attempt to compensate in amounts fixed by a statutory "schedule" for the loss or the loss of the use of specific body parts. The schedules of most U.S. jurisdictions include specified amounts for loss of arm, hand, digits of the hand, leg, foot, toes, eye, hearing in one ear, and hearing in both ears. There are, of course, exceptions:

- Puerto Rico has a special provision for loss of one eye.
- Idaho, Louisiana, Michigan, and Texas do not have provision for loss of hearing in one ear. Louisiana, Michigan, and Wyoming have no scheduled provision for total loss of hearing in both ears. Nor does Nebraska, but it treats this impairment as presumed permanent and total disability.
- Massachusetts' schedule includes only loss of arm, hand, leg, foot, eye, hearing of one ear and total loss of hearing.

- Georgia, Minnesota, and Nevada have no schedules at all—those states provide for only non-scheduled permanent partial disability, and claimants in those states who suffer from such injuries are required to establish on a case-by-case basis the percentage of partial disability or impairment that they suffer.

Most states with scheduled-loss compensation allow such awards in addition to compensation for temporary total disability, but Indiana, Kansas, New York, and Pennsylvania have limitations on the period of time for collecting both awards.

The U.S. Chamber of Commerce Chart, "Income Benefits for Scheduled Injuries," Appendix E, provides a jurisdiction-by-jurisdiction breakdown.

DEATH BENEFITS

Weekly compensation benefits are paid to surviving dependents—typically children and spouses—of workers who are killed in the course of employment or as the result of a work-related injury or occupational disease in all U.S. jurisdictions. Death benefits to a surviving spouse usually end upon remarriage. A few states provide a lump-sum award if the surviving spouse remarries. Death benefits for surviving children end when they reach majority or, if they are full-time students, continue until age 21, 23, or 25.

Amounts are limited in weekly rate and in duration. The typical death-benefit provision is weekly compensation of 66 and two-thirds percent of the deceased worker's average weekly wage up to a maximum of 100 percent of the statewide average weekly wage but not below a minimum of a fixed amount, say, $25.00. Arizona, Iowa, Minnesota, Missouri, and Nevada have no floors on the weekly benefit.

The range of benefits is astonishing. Alaska's maximum weekly benefit of 200 percent of statewide average weekly wage amounts to virtually no ceiling. In contrast, Mississippi's maximum of $140 for a surviving spouse and children seems designed to keep unfortunate widows and surviving children securely beneath the poverty line.

About a third of the states still provide an amount limit on the total death award, and a few provide time limits stated as a fixed number of weeks or years of compensation.

See U.S. Chamber of Commerce Chart, "Fatalities—Income Benefits for Spouse and Children," Appendix D, for a breakdown of the various states and U.S. jurisdictions.

MEDICAL BENEFITS

In all U.S. jurisdictions except the Virgin Islands there is no limitation on medical coverage for conditions that result from allowed injuries or occupational diseases. Medical coverage includes costs or fees of physicians, hospitals, required nursing service (including home nursing service), physical therapy, dentists, chiropractors, and prosthetic devices. Many states provide for replacement eyeglasses, and a few states even provide recognition for prayer or spiritual treatment.

6

JURISDICTION AND PROCEDURE

The jurisdiction of state workers' compensation agencies is strictly limited by the terms of statutes that created them. This partly explains why a significant number of judicial decisions have strictly construed laws governing limitations periods, intra-agency review, and other statutes limiting the jurisdiction of workers' compensation agencies in apparent disregard of the usual rule that workers' compensation laws are to be liberally construed in favor of claimants or in favor of coverage.

As a threshold matter, a state's workers' compensation law can be applicable only to those employer-employee relationships that are under the control of the state's governmental power. This generally means that there must be sufficient contacts between the employment and the state for the state to assume jurisdiction (e.g., the employee and the employer are located in the state) and that federal legislation has not preempted the field (e.g., an injured harbor worker, covered under the federal Longshore and Harborworker's Compensation Act, is not entitled to state workers' compensation benefits).

State agencies exercise several types of jurisdiction over workers' compensation claims. In those jurisdictions that have a state insurance fund, particularly those states with monopolistic state funds, it is sometimes said that a state agency needs "jurisdiction to make payment." To practitioners in jurisdictions without state funds this may seem like an odd choice of words but, on analysis, the usage is both meaningful and sound. The state agency is a creature of statute and, like a board that hears disputed claims, it has no powers other than those conferred by the statute.

More in keeping with general usage, the term "quasi-adjudicatory jurisdiction of state agencies" describes the power of the board, bureau, or commission to hear and render decisions in disputed claims or to resolve other workers' compensation issues. This sort of jurisdiction can be divided into the power to hear and resolve disputes and the power to modify decisions.

Virtually all agencies have the power to issue regulations or rules for enforcement, procedure, and interpretation of the local workers' compensation act. Regulations that are properly promulgated, i.e., in accordance with applicable administrative procedures, are binding and have the force of law so long as they are reasonable and consistent with the underlying statutes.

The state agency is almost always given general power over the workers' compensation system. This power includes the authority to investigate claims, to collect and disburse funds, to employ sufficient staff to perform its statutory duties, and to compel employers and insurance carriers to comply with the workers' compensation act.

Before an agency can assert jurisdiction over a matter, certain conditions must be met. The most common ones include institution of proceedings and filing of a claim with the state agency within the statutorily imposed time limitations, and a demonstrated inability by the claimant to affect a voluntary agreement with the employer or insurance carrier.

In most jurisdictions, satisfying the requisite statute of limitations is mandatory. Limitations periods in this area of law are distinguished from general statutes of limitations. Some courts, such as the North Carolina Supreme Court *(McCrater v. Stone & Webster Eng'g Corp.)* and an Indiana appellate court *(Warinchak v. United States Steel Corp.)* have refused even to apply the term "statute of limitations" to them at all, preferring to describe them as "nonclaim" statutes or simply, "a condition annexed to a right."

Although strict application of limitations periods appears to be relaxing somewhat, it remains the case that statutes of limitations must be complied with and failure to file a claim within the limitations period generally will not be excused even if the result of ignorance of the existence of the claim, lunacy, infancy, imprisonment, or other reason that might toll a general statute of limitations.

A few judicial decisions, most notably those of the Ohio Supreme Court in *Greenwalt v. Goodyear Tire & Rubber Co.*, and the U.S. Court of Appeals for the Ninth Circuit (applying Alaska territorial law) in *Hilty v. Fairbanks Exploration Co.*, went so far as to hold that failure to file timely will not be excused even if the failure is caused by outright fraud by an employer. This extreme and distinctly minority view appears to be of dubious viability in at least one of those jurisdictions—it was questioned in the Ohio appellate decision, *Delamotte v. Unitcast Div. of Midland-Ross Corp.*

A growing number of cases are recognizing an exception to strict construction of statutes of limitations if the elements of waiver or estoppel are shown. Waiver or estoppel apply when the action of an employer or insurance carrier has induced an employee's failure to file a claim, as for example, in *Molex v. Industrial Comm'n* when an employer lulled an injured worker into a false sense of security by promising to "take care" of him or his claim. The Illinois Supreme Court held that under such circumstances an employer can lose its right to assert a statute of limitations as a defense against the claim.

CONFLICT OF LAWS

Conflicts With Federal Jurisdiction

As has already been noted, state workers' compensation systems have been preempted by federal maritime and admiralty jurisdiction under the Longshore and Harborworkers Compensation Act and the Federal Employees' Compensation Act. Interstate commerce, over which Congress has plenary power under the U.S. Constitution, has received different treatment, however. The U.S. Supreme Court in *Valley S.S. Co. v.*

Jensen held that a state has power to provide workers' compensation coverage unless the U.S. Congress exercised preemption rights.

More specifically, the Court in *Gilvary v. Cuyahoga V.R. Co.* held that a state lawfully asserted jurisdiction over a claim against an employer who was engaged in both interstate and intrastate business. *Gilvary* held that the claim could be subject to state coverage, even if Congress has established a method of compensation, where the following conditions were met:

- the intrastate work is clearly separable and distinguishable from the interstate (or foreign) commerce;
- the "separable" work, for its duration, is performed in the state;
- the employer and employee voluntarily accept coverage in the state;
- the state agency approves the coverage; and
- no act of Congress forbids such coverage.

Whether federal coverage obtains is determined by decisions of federal courts. *Moore v. Indus. Comm'n* (Ohio).

Federal labor law does not pre-empt state workers' compensation actions. See *Lingle v. Norge Div. of Magic Chef* (U.S. Sup. Ct.).

Minimal Contacts with Forum State

In order for a state to assert jurisdiction over a claim, certain minimal contacts must be established. Some courts will look to the "totality of facts" surrounding a work-related injury or disease to determine whether "minimal contacts" have been met; however, they appear to treat certain factors as more important than others. The occurrence of a work-related injury in a state is generally the most important single factor, although the locus of the contract of hire is also quite significant. Other factors in the calculus include the place of the claimant's residency, the principal place of employment, the employer's principal place of business, the amount of work to be performed in the state, and the duration of employment within the state.

The threshold questions of minimal contacts and federal

preemption relate primarily to the jurisdiction of a particular local government over a claim, or, put another way, to whether the local government has the lawful power to assert the coverage of a particular claim by its laws. However, the mere fact that a state *could* assert power over a particular injury or claim does not mean that the state *must* assert such jurisdiction. Moreover, even if a state does have jurisdiction and, by applying its own laws, finds that it will cover a claim or injury, it does not necessarily follow that the laws of other states are thereby precluded from covering it. In *Alaska Packers Ass'n v. Industrial Accident Comm'n*, the U.S. Supreme Court held that a state's workers' compensation act was not rendered inapplicable merely because another state's workers' compensation act also applied.

Nevertheless, if it is established by the state in which the claim is filed ("forum state") that the compensation act of another jurisdiction controls, the local court usually will give effect to the foreign act either under the doctrine of comity or under rules governing the enforcement of contractual rights. In the event of conflicting or overlapping jurisdictions, rules of law which give preference to the local jurisdiction appear to be enforceable. And most states have provision for write-offs of compensation received under the workers' compensation laws of another jurisdiction.

Opinions vary so widely in their approaches to choice of law where several states might have jurisdiction that, with one obverse exception, few general principles can be said to be useful: the fact that a particular claim will *not* be covered anywhere else has been acknowledged as an important factor in a determination by courts to accept local coverage over a claim.

The place of injury is sometimes said to be the most important factor but the states show little agreement on even this point. Consider:

- The law of place of injury was held to be controlling for choice-of-law purposes over the law of state in which employment contract was consummated by the Connecticut Supreme Court *(Douthwright v. Champlin)*, the Michigan Supreme Court *(Cline v. Byrne Doors, Inc.)*, and the Wisconsin Supreme Court *(Salvation Army v. Industrial Comm'n)*.

- But the Ohio Supreme Court *(Spohn v. Industrial Comm'n)* and an Indiana appeals court *(Darsch v. Thearle Duffield Fireworks Display Co.)* refused to apply the law of the forum in which the injury took place when other indicia of minimal contacts with that state were absent.

Statutory Provisions

While the provisions of a state's statutes are relevant in determining the proper forum, they are not controlling, since the threshold issue is whether the transaction or occurrence has sufficient contacts with the state such that the state's fundamental power over it arises. Thus, although an Ohio statute appears to make it impossible for anyone who "enters . . . a contract of hire" in Ohio to be free of Ohio coverage, the Ohio Supreme Court ruled in *Industrial Comm'n of Ohio v. Gardinio* that Ohio coverage could not attach if no part of an employment contract was to be performed in the state, even if the contract were "entered into" in Ohio.

Statutes describing coverage vary widely. Alabama and Hawaii are typical of states that provide for local coverage if the contract of employment is entered into locally. California makes this one factor in determining coverage. Michigan's law contains a provision similar to California's but its supreme court has construed the provision to mandate coverage if the contract of employment is entered into in the state. *(Roberts v. I.X.L. Glass Corp., Wearner v. West Michigan Conference of Seventh Day Adventists.)*

Although the statutes of most states prevent double recovery by providing for a credit of any compensation paid under the workers' compensation laws of another state for the same injury, a Michigan appellate decision suggests that there is no constitutional bar to double recovery. *(Adams v. Emery Transp. Co.)* But the U.S. Supreme Court in *Magnolia Petroleum Co. v. Hunt* and *Wisconsin v. McMartin* states that an award by one state that is intended to be final and conclusive of all the employee's rights against the employer and the insurer is binding on another.

JURISDICTION TO HEAR DISPUTES

When a claim is disputed or controverted and an agreement cannot be reached between the claimant and the employer or insurance carrier, the dispute is heard by the state agency. In this quasi-adjudicatory capacity, the agency makes findings of fact and rulings of law. The power of a state workers' compensation agency to hear disputes is limited by the terms of the applicable state statute and by due process of law and other constitutional restrictions.

Statutes Conferring Jurisdiction

Statutes granting to the state agencies the power to hear disputes are narrowly construed. The Supreme Court of Mississippi in *L.&A. Constr. Co. v. McCharen* expressed a widely accepted rule that parties have no power to confer jurisdiction upon such agencies by stipulation or to waive jurisdictional objections by agreement.

A state agency has only such powers as are expressly granted by statute or as are necessarily implied by such express grants. An agency vested with power to hear workers' compensation disputes cannot hear other kinds of controversies. The California Supreme Court announced this general rule in *Yosemite Lumber Co. v. Industrial Accident Comm'n*. However, resolution of issues that are necessary incidents to other powers granted—for example, an employer's amenability or insurance coverage, or the agency's assertion of authority to order a self-insured employer to make a payment *(Utah Cooper Co. v. Industrial Comm'n)*—will be upheld as "clearly implied," even if such power was not expressly granted by statute.

Due Process

The jurisdiction of state agencies over disputed claims is also limited by constitutional restrictions. The relative informality of workers' compensation proceedings and the relaxation of the applicable rules of evidence (which the U.S. Supreme Court has held does not in itself violate due process, *Crowell v. Benson*) permit agencies to handle and resolve large numbers of claims expeditiously. But when such agencies make findings of fact and legal conclusions in disputes between parties, they act in a judicial capacity and, therefore, are required to meet due process standards.

Due process requirements include

- reasonable notice to parties affected by the dispute,
- fairness and impartiality in the hearing, and
- factual findings based on probative evidence.

A good general discussion of these principles appears in the Idaho Supreme Court decision of *Cook v. Massey*.

Notice

Reasonable notice generally means that the parties are provided information regarding the date, the time, and the place of hearing and the specific issue presented. It also means that the parties have sufficient time in which to prepare for the hearing. Notice received "one to three days" before the hearing has recently been held by a Florida appellate court to be insufficient. *(Security Aluminum Windows v. Smith.)* Although orders issued without notice at any stage of the administrative proceedings are void as violations of due process, a party may waive the notice requirement either orally or in writing.

Fairness

Any administrative hearing that is not fair, open, and impartial is also void as a violation of due process. Impartiality means that the triers of fact or hearing officers have no personal benefit in the outcome and have expressed no opinion on the ultimate conclusion before hearing the evidence.

Moreover, triers of fact should not be related by blood or marriage to the litigants or their attorneys. Applying this rule, a Texas appellate court declared invalid an award issued by a judge who was the first cousin of the wife of a member of the law firm representing one of the parties. *(Texas Employers' Ins. Ass'n v. Scroggins.)*

Although the hearing should be before the individuals who make the decision, *Wozniak's Case* (Mass.) stands for the general proposition that a mere change in the membership on the board that heard the case does not render a decision void so long as the remaining original members who concur constitute a majority of the board's quorum.

A workers' compensation statute does not violate due process of law merely because it provides for no administrative review or rehearing. The hearing is adequate if it affords all parties the opportunity to be heard and to present evidence and cross-examine or otherwise challenge opposing evidence.

Evidence in the Record

All material facts relied upon by the trier of fact must be put in the record and must be supported by evidence. Orders not meeting this requirement have been described as "arbitrary" and are therefore invalid. The Kentucky Supreme Court's opinion in *American Beauty Homes Corp. v. Louisville & Jefferson County Planning & Zoning Comm'n* contains a good general discussion of this requirement.

JURISDICTION TO MODIFY A FINAL ORDER

Although an administrative agency is not a court of general jurisdiction, it does possess some powers that are equitable in nature to modify its unappealed decisions. These powers include the power to revoke final orders* induced through fraud, to correct for clerical mistakes, and to modify non-final orders.

In addition to these equitable powers or powers inherent in an agency's functions as a decision-maker, most states make statutory provision for continuing jurisdiction to modify awards.

* The discussion assumes the accepted definition of "final order": an order conclusively resolving a dispute issued by an agency of competent jurisdiction either for which there exists no appeal, review, or reconsideration, or from which no appeal or request for review or reconsideration has been taken by any aggrieved party within the prescribed time limits.

Fraud

It is uniformly accepted that an administrative agency has the power to modify or revoke any award that was induced through fraud. This power is said to be inherent in the agency whose jurisdiction was befouled and is not controlled by the conditions or limitations period imposed by a statute providing for modification of final awards. Hence, an agency may revoke a fraudulently induced order at any time, even if it has otherwise lost jurisdiction over a claim because of the running of the limitations period contained in a continuing jurisdiction statute.

The definitions of fraud vary, but generally to establish a case of fraud, in order to revoke a decision of an administrative agency, the following elements must be present:

- The making of a material false statement with knowledge of its falsity, or concealment or suppression of a material truth when there is a duty to disclose;
- intent in either case to deceive;
- the right by another party to rely upon the false statement or nondisclosure;
- actual reliance on the false statement or nondisclosure, which results in inducement to action or injurious change of position; and
- damages or injury.

The party alleging fraud must establish each element by clear and convincing evidence. *Dapsco, Inc. v. Dependent of Upchurch* (Miss.) discusses the basic power of workers' compensation agencies to revoke fraudulently induced orders.

Discovery of Error

While some courts have come out strongly against modification of final orders, it is a fairly well accepted practice for agencies to modify awards that are discovered to have been based upon mistakes of fact.

Clerical mistakes or mistakes in computation are universally recognized as proper grounds for invoking the power to modify awards. Another sort of easily ascertainable mistake that falls into this category is the issuance of an award by an agency to the wrong person. The Ohio Supreme Court was presented with an interesting variation on this latter category in *Industrial Comm'n v. Dell.* In this case, a death claim was granted by the commission to a woman claiming to be the surviving spouse of a killed worker. The commission revoked the award when the real widow was discovered, and its modification was upheld by the court.

Decisions in cases involving those sorts of errors that are not so easily capable of ascertainment are not unanimous in allowing modifications. An Ohio appellate court, for example, refused to permit the Ohio Industrial Commission to reconsider a final decision despite the "excellence of medical evidence" that was presented at the later hearing. *(Oberlin v. Industrial Comm'n.)* A Texas appeals court, faced with a similar factual situation, permitted modification. *(Twin City Fire Ins. Co. v. Foster.)*

The obvious tension in these decisions stems from two important principles. The first is that controversies must come to an end sometime; at some point, there must be a final decision. The second is that decisions—particularly decisions by administrative agencies—should be reopened on occasion in the interest of justice or the appearance of justice. The debate over whether the judicial doctrines related to finality—res judicata and collateral estoppel—should apply to decisions of workers' compensation administrative bodies is resolving in favor of their application, although, as the U.S. Supreme Court noted, the doctrines may surface under other names, "claim preclusion" and "issue preclusion." *(Migra v. Warren School Dist. Bd. of Ed.)*

The questions and policy considerations regarding review of final awards remain: When, notwithstanding the important considerations embodied in the concept of res judicata, do circumstances justify reexamination of an issue? It is clear that even broadly worded statutes for review or modification will not afford a party a rehearing of a final decision if there is no new evidence or no discovery of error. In short, once the appeal period has passed on a final decision, the adjudicating body has no power simply to change its mind on the import of evidence that was already before it.

Adjudicating bodies do have the power to modify nonfinal orders, however. And an order that indicates that the tribunal is taking the matter under advisement or ordering additional medical evidence may be modified at a later time by the tribunal and a final order entered thereafter.

PROCEDURES

The procedures used in workers' compensation systems vary markedly; however, some general characteristics are common among them. Procedures in all workers' compensation systems are designed to be as informal as possible, and, therefore, technical rules regarding pleadings, documentation, and claims processing are avoided as much as possible.

The processing of a high volume of claims necessarily requires a heavy dependence by the workers' compensation agencies on forms. Claimants, insurers, and employers working with the system should become familiar with the forms of their state and should know how to complete them, where to file them, what documentation should accompany them, and what follow-ups they require. It should be noted, however, that while the proper use of forms will expedite virtually any application, failure to use a proper form generally is not sufficient reason for an agency to deny a request or application.

Most states provide for a mode of intra-agency review or rehearing. Sometimes the higher administrative tribunal—which may consist of a board of several commissioners, deputies, or administrative law judges, rather than the single hearing officer who usually presides at the first-level hearing—has somewhat more impressive procedures. But these are usually more matters of form than of substance and the relaxed rules of evidence still will usually obtain.

Unlike changes in substantive laws, changes in procedural laws may be made applicable to pending proceedings. Statutes of limitations generally are considered to be substantive in this field, however, and are fixed as of the date of the injury, disability, or death. On the other hand, changes in the method of intra-agency review are procedural and a change in such a law will apply to claims pending before the agency. (See *Anderson v. Minnesota ex rel. General Accident & Life Assurance Corp.*)

POWER TO OVERSEE SYSTEM

In addition to the above specific grants of jurisdiction, workers' compensation agencies are generally given a plenary power to oversee the system—a power that is especially articulate in state-fund jurisdictions. Included in this general power may be express grants, such as the power to approve settlements between claimants and self-insured employers or private insurance carriers in addition to settlements with the state fund, and implied grants, such as the power that exists regardless of specific statutory grant to investigate claims, allegations of fraud, safety violations by employers, and noncompliance by employers or insurance companies.

Virtually all workers' compensation agencies have the power to issue regulations. So long as these regulations are issued pursuant to statutory procedure, are consistent with the workers' compensation act of the state, and are reasonable, they will be upheld by courts, even when they work hardship on individual parties.

7
ADMINISTRATION

THE AGENCIES

Specific agencies of one kind or another—industrial commissions, bureaus or offices of workers' compensation, industrial accident boards, boards of workers' compensation appeals—exist in most U.S. jurisdictions to administer workers' compensation systems. (A listing of federal and state workers' compensation administrative agencies is provided in Appendix H.) The jurisdiction or power of these agencies to act has been discussed in the previous chapter. This chapter is concerned with methods of administering the various workers' compensation systems.

Court-administered Systems

Louisiana, Alabama, New Mexico, Tennessee, and Wyoming have court-administered workers' compensation systems. Louisiana vests *all* administrative functions in its courts. The other states mentioned have set up some sort of agency for ministerial or statistic-gathering purposes. W.S. Malone, M.L. Plant, and J.W. Little in WORKERS' COMPENSATION AND EMPLOYMENT RIGHTS have articulated the problems with court administration of workers' compensation systems and along the way provided a good listing of the functions usually thought of as "administrative" in the workers' compensation context:

> "Courts are simply not equipped to do the job required for workers' compensation to be effective. Injured workers need help in

the early stages of their distress and a properly functioning administrative agency sees that it is provided. A court on the other hand must await the initiative of the parties. Courts do not have the facilities or staff for keeping files on cases, following up initial determinations of disability, insuring prompt payments, keeping statistics, publishing information needed by both employer and employees, and performing the many other tasks that must be done if the compensation statute is to function effectively."

The inadequacies of court administration are becoming known and a trend away from that form of administration is developing. In New Mexico, however, the decision in *State v. Mechem* may impose a state-constitutional impediment to completely eliminating it.

Functions of Administrative Agencies

The National Commission on State Workmen's Compensation Laws identified six primary obligations of workers' compensation programs:

- Taking the initiative in administering the law;
- Continually reviewing the performance of the program with a willingness to change its procedures and to request the state legislature to make needed amendments;
- Advising workers of their rights and obligations and assuring that they receive the benefits to which they are entitled;
- Apprising employers and carriers of their rights and obligations; informing other parties in the delivery system such as health-care providers of their obligations and privileges;
- Assisting in voluntary and informal resolution of disputes that are consistent with law and prohibiting inappropriate agreements;
- Adjudicating claims that cannot be resolved voluntarily.

Waiting Period

Injured workers are not entitled to temporary total disability or other types of compensation unless they have lost a specified period of time from work. The purpose of the waiting period is to exclude minor injuries from being treated as lost-time claims and to avoid excessive costs and overhead. The waiting period, which does not apply to medical benefits, is now a week or less throughout the U.S.

DISPUTE RESOLUTION

When workers' compensation disputes arise they may be resolved at the administrative level of hearing officers, administrative law judges, referees, deputies, commissioners, administrators, or through arbitration. Many states have adopted a dispute-resolution system which is independent of the other administrative functions and which permits appeal of a hearing officer's initial decision to a separate agency review or appeals board. This approach has the advantages of keeping the perfunctory administrative activities from becoming bogged down with disputed claims and assuring the independence of the adjudicatory officers.

The provision of separate means of dispute resolution within an agency is growing in acceptance across the country and was described with apparent approval by The National Commission on State Workmen's Compensation Laws as being ". . . in accord with the recommendation of the Council of State Governments." The Commission recommended the approach in its 1972 Report.

(For a discussion of dispute resolution by review or appeal of an administrative hearing by court, see Chapter 8.)

Burden of Proof

The claimant has the general burden of proving entitlement to compensation. Although the rules of evidence generally do not apply to administrative hearings in workers' compensation, proof supporting the claimant's case must be relevant and probative. Proof of known and obvious facts is not necessary, however, since the doctrine of judicial notice applies in these proceedings.

A few courts have applied the spirit of liberal construction here. The Utah Supreme Court, for example, held that "in case there is doubt . . . such doubt should be resolved in favor of the employee. . . ." *(Chandler v. Industrial Comm'n of Utah.)* Similar language appears in *Western Electric Co. v. Workers' Compensation Appeals Bd.* (Cal.) and *Cooper v. Industrial Comm'n* (Ohio). Considering the weight of authority clearly stating that the claimant bears the burden of proof, however, these cases might be best viewed as *suggestions* to administrative agencies rather than as rules of law.

The burden of proof with regard to specific matters may not always be on the claimant, as the following examples show:

- *Status as independent contractor.* There is a three-way split as to which party bears the burden when this issue is raised. Some courts, like the Maine Supreme Court in *Murray's Case,* say that the putative employer has the burden to establish that the claimant was not an employee; others, such as the Texas Court of Civil Appeals in *Guzman v. Aetna Casualty & Surety Co.,* place the burden on the claimant; while others, for example, the Ohio Supreme Court in *Industrial Comm'n v. Laird,* skirt the burden-of-proof issue by saying that, once the issue is raised, there is no presumption either way.
- *Unexplained cause of injury or death.* Workers who are found injured or dead at a worksite are sometimes presumed to have been injured or killed in the course of their employment when no explanation can be offered for the cause of the injury or death. This presumption is a product of the common-law presumptions against suicide and murder and the rule of liberal construction of workers' compensation statutes. Thus, in the New York case of *Slotnick v. Howard Stores Corp.,* a worker who was found after sustaining an unwitnessed mugging was held entitled to compensation.

  But in *Chaudier v. Stearns & Culver Lumber Co.,* the Michigan Supreme Court ruled noncompensable the death of a furnace cleaner killed by a cupful of ashes he swallowed. The circumstantial evidence of the effort required to swallow so much ash was held to rebut the presumption against suicide.

- *Fault of employee as bar to compensability.* The employer usually bears the burden of proving this as an affirmative defense. (*King v. Empire Collieries Co.* (Va.).)
- *Fraud.* The burden of proof is on the party alleging fraud and the degree of proof required is clear and convincing evidence. (See Chapter 6.)
- *Presumptions imposed by statute.* These vary from state to state. A by no means exhaustive list includes:

  Employees who are engaged in specified occupations and who contract "scheduled diseases" are entitled to a presumption of causation. (See Chapter 3.) In *Permanente Medical Group v. Workers' Compensation Appeals Bd.*, a California appellate court held this statutory presumption to be rebuttable.

  Surviving spouses and minor children who are living with the deceased worker at the time of death or who are legally entitled to support from the worker are presumed to be dependent. (See Chapter 4.) Statutes sometimes make the presumption conclusive. However, the constitutionality of providing conclusive presumptions for widows but rebuttable presumptions for widowers is uncertain. Such a statute was struck down by the California Supreme Court on equal protection grounds in *Arp v. Workers' Compensation Appeals Bd.*, but a similar statute was upheld by the Missouri Supreme Court. *(Wengler v. Druggists Mutual Ins. Co.)* An Ohio appellate decision upheld a distinction granting a *rebuttable* presumption, i.e., a shift in the usual burden of going forward, to widows but not to widowers: "Were such presumption conclusive, perhaps there would be merit to (widower-claimant's) contention . . ." that it violated Equal Protection. *(Lee v. Daugherty.)*

  Reduction in weekly wages after the date of injury sometimes creates a presumption of loss of earning capacity. (See Chapter 5.)

With the bright-line exception of fraud, the degree of proof required throughout workers' compensation claims is a preponderance of the evidence.

PARTIES

Since workers' compensation is a statutory scheme and all rights and benefits are limited by statute, common-law rules with respect to parties have little application. It's best to begin with this negative observation and keep it in mind: no one is a party to a workers' compensation claim, proceeding, or lawsuit unless the applicable workers' compensation statute implicitly or expressly so provides.

Statutes and regulations permit claimants, employers, insurance carriers, and, sometimes a representative from the non-adjudicatory administrative board or state insurance fund to be parties to administrative hearings. On appeal or other court review of the administrative decision, the adjudicatory agency that made the decision is usually allowed, and sometimes is required, to be a party.

Minors who are injured in the course of employment usually may maintain their own actions in their own names. Similarly, minor children of deceased employees may be entitled to assert their own survivor claims, particularly if their rights are not connected to the rights of a surviving parent.

AGREEMENTS AND SETTLEMENTS

This section is confined to agreements between the claimant and the employer in contested claims. (A certified or uncontested claim* is one on which the employer or carrier and the claimant agree as to liability and, in that sense, is an agreement.) There are various kinds of agreements between claimants and employers or insurance carriers regarding workers' compensation liability. Some of the agreements—waivers of statutory rights—are void or voidable. Others—agreements regarding liability, which in effect are admissions of compensability—generally are bilateral in the sense that both sides are

---

* It is worth noting that most claims are uncontested and most requests for compensation are paid voluntarily. W.S. MALONE, M.L. PLANT, J.W. LITTLE, WORKERS' COMPENSATION AND EMPLOYMENT RIGHTS, CASES AND MATERIALS at 402-403 (2d ed. 1982) says that 70–90 percent of claims entail no dispute of fact or law. THE REPORT OF THE NATIONAL COMMISSION ON STATE WORKMEN'S COMPENSATION LAW (Table 6.1) (1972) reported that, in 17 of 25 states for which estimates could be made, contested cases amounted to less than 10 percent or all reported cases.

free to enter the agreement without supervision. (In the event that no agreement as to liability is reached, the claim or issue usually goes before the quasi-adjudicatory administrative agency for resolution.) Still other agreements—settlements, stipulations, compromises, or advancements—usually require the approval of a state agency. As has been noted in Chapter 6, however, an agreement between an employee and employer or carrier cannot vest jurisdiction over a claim in a state agency.

An employee's purported waiver of rights to workers' compensation is an invalid agreement. "Waiver" in this context means an agreement by a worker to release an employer from liability for workers' compensation claims *before the worker's right to compensation has accrued,* by for example, a blanket release from liability signed when a worker begins employment. But this does not mean that, once the rights have accrued, after the injury or death has occurred or the occupational disease has been contracted and after the jurisdiction of the state workers' compensation agencies has been invoked, the parties cannot agree to a compromise or settlement.

Although in theory, settlements and agreements are relatively easy to understand, some confusion results from differing use of the terms in different jurisdictions. Settlement of a claim usually means a complete discharge by the claimant of any liability on the part of the employer or insurance carrier for all costs in the claim, including all compensation, fees, and other benefits, in exchange for a lump sum of money. Some states have policies against complete settlement of claims unless there is a showing that the claimant has other sources of medical coverage.

An individual who has several potential causes of action against an employer may enter into a settlement that is so broad as to preclude a workers' compensation claim. In *Ho v. Martin Marietta,* the U.S. Court of Appeals for the Fifth Circuit ruled that a settlement in an employment-discrimination suit of "all actions, claims or lawsuits whatsoever" prevented a claimant from filing for workers' compensation.

The federal court in which the discrimination action was brought would not have had jurisdiction over the compensation claim in *Ho,* and state-mandated procedures for workers' compensation settlements were not followed. Nevertheless, *Ho* held that the settlement agreement should be analyzed as a contract between disputing parties and not just in terms of the rights that were being litigated before the court. Since the parties to the settlement were free to "agree to any terms not opposed to public policy" their agreement to settle out all future state and federal claims was binding.

A stipulation is a formal agreement that usually requires approval of the state agency. A stipulation differs from a settlement in that it is an agreement as to only specified issues. It is not a release from liability.

Thus for example, an employer who contests part of John Doe's claim may enter into an agreement that John was injured in the course of employment and that he was temporarily and totally disabled for one month. This agreement is a stipulation, and it leaves open the possibility that John may be disabled for additional periods after the month. New periods of disability may be addressed in future agreements or in hearings brought before the state agency.

On the other hand, if the employer wishes to settle the claim, it may offer John a lump sum and, in exchange, John will agree not to pursue any rights under the claim.

Partial settlement means a discharge of only part of the liability—say, liability for compensation only—for a lump sum of money, without a release of liability for the remaining segments of the claim, e.g., medical bills. Many state agencies, based on administrative considerations, refuse to approve partial settlement of claims, even where there is no legal impediment to them.

A lump-sum advancement, on the other hand, is a commutation to present value of part of an allowed claim. Often advancements are granted against claims paying long-term or indefinite compensation, i.e., permanent and total disability or death claims, for the purpose of making large purchases, investments, or to pay for education or training. Advancements are also routinely used to pay for attorney's fees in some states. Payments of a lump sum advancement are usually made by a single check; prorated amounts are thereafter deducted from the claimant's weekly benefits, based upon the life expectancy of the claimant or upon the expected duration of the weekly benefit.

Most states provide that settlements or stipulations may not be made without approval of the state agency. Some states provide specific circumstances in which settlements are permitted. In the absence of such provisions, most states refuse to honor settlements that are less than the compensation specified in the statute. Others let the parties work out their own agreements as they see fit. Often, even in those states that normally discourage settlements, settlements of claims are encouraged once the claims have been appealed in court.

Two sets of conflicting policies are reflected in this split of authority. On the one hand, claimants—injured workers who often have been out of work and are attempting to secure compensation in a contested claim and may be in financial difficulties—should be protected from the unequal bargaining power of employers or insurance carriers who can afford to offer a significant-sounding sum of money in exchange for statutory rights designed to provide long-term, perhaps lifetime, protection. Moreover, since a specific purpose of workers' compensation is the continuing protection of the worker, permitting compromises of these rights through lump-sum settlements goes against the basic design of the plan.

On the other hand, workers are capable of making their own decisions and their decisions should be respected. In addition, compromises and settlements are great aids in administration of workers' compensation and are a good way of ridding the system of contested claims.

A settlement of less than the amount specified in the statute was held void by the Washington Supreme Court in *Southern v. Department of Labor and Indus.*, while the Kansas Supreme Court in *Dotson v. Procter & Gamble Mfg. Co.* refused to set aside a settlement agreement under similar circumstances. The New Jersey Supreme Court decision, *Nagy v. Ford Motor Co.*, contains a good discussion of policy considerations supporting the state's active involvement in the settlement process.

8 JUDICIAL REVIEW

ISSUES REVIEWABLE BY COURT

Virtually all states provide for some judicial review of final administrative decisions. A slight majority of those states permit review of only issues of law, a policy endorsed by the National Commission on State Workmen's Compensation Laws which stated in its 1972 Report: "We recommend that where there is an appellate level within the workmen's compensation agency, the decisions of the workmen's compensation agency be reviewed by courts only on questions of law."

In states that do not permit appeal of questions of fact, it is generally recognized that factual issues can nevertheless be attacked on the ground that a finding was made without supporting evidence. Such a finding is said to be "arbitrary," "capricious," or "an abuse of discretion," and, therefore, correctable under general authority vested in courts or under courts' power to oversee administrative procedures.

This power does not permit the reviewing court to reweigh the evidence in factual issues however, and if inferences from the proof in the record can reasonably support the administrative finding, that finding generally will not be disturbed.

The U.S. Supreme Court has held that the failure of a workers' compensation system to provide judicial review on questions of fact does not violate due process *(Hawkins v. Bleakly)*. The Court also held that a finding and decision of a state administrative body upon a question of fact, affirmed by state courts, is conclusive upon federal courts unless the finding is ascertained to be without evidentiary support. *(Ward & Gow v. Krinsky, U.S. Sup. Ct.)*

Conclusions of Fact and of Law

The distinction between conclusions that are supposedly legal and findings that are supposedly factual is not exactly a bright line in many cases. Exceptions, qualifications, and inconsistent applications of the terms are not unusual.

Of course, the legal conclusions that are based upon facts are fully reviewable in court as are all questions of law. The following hypothetical example of findings made in a decision rendered by an administrative agency in a jurisdiction whose statutes purport to permit appeal from only questions of law, provides an illustration of the distinction between a factual finding and a legal conclusion:

1. On September 9, John Claimant, a janitor, was sweeping the floor of XYZ Co., doing his regular work in the regular way;
2. John saw something shiny on the floor amid the sweepings. John believed that the shiny object was an important widget that was needed by his supervisor;
3. As he bent over to pick up the object he felt a severe pain in his lower back;
4. As a result of this incident, John sustained an acute lower back sprain;
5. John did not sustain an "accident" as defined by the laws of this state;
6. Therefore John's claim is disallowed.

Findings one through four in this decision are findings of fact and, if there is supporting evidence for them, will not be disturbed by the reviewing court. Finding five, however, should be considered a conclusion of law, that is, an interpretation of a statutory term, and is subject to full review by the court. Accordingly, finding six, disallowing the claim, may also be set aside if the reviewing court disagrees with the agency as to finding five.

Applying these standards of review on a case-by-case basis leads to some difficulty, even though articulating the general rule may seem easy enough. The Idaho Supreme Court, for instance, applied what it perceived to be the majority view in *Re Haynes*. It recognized the general rule that the factual issue of dependency is not normally reviewable by a court, but reversed an order denying benefits to a widow-claimant. The court held that the evidence established that the claimant had relied on decedent's support and help and, therefore, was entitled to benefits.

A narrow approach to judicial review is represented by *Gentry v. State Indus. Comm'n*, in which the Oklahoma Supreme Court refused to review an administrative determination that a claimant had suffered an accidental injury.

Having stated that questions of law are generally reviewable is only to introduce the main problem encountered in this context. A complicated division of opinion exists as to what constitutes a factual finding and what constitutes a legal ruling. The problem is compounded by labeling certain questions as "mixed." The following issues illustrate some of the problems:

- "Findings of fact upon which the agency's jurisdiction is based" are sometimes said to be reviewable even in the absence of statutory authority to review questions of fact. This is a confused and confusing exception for several reasons. First, this generally stated exception fails to differentiate between the various kinds of jurisdiction that an agency possesses. (See Chapter 6.)

  Moreover, if it is taken literally this exception could encompass just about any finding of fact made by the agency. For example, findings of injury, existence of the employee-employer relationship, and work-relatedness of the injury are all necessary before a state agency can assert continuing jurisdiction or jurisdiction to make payment or to oversee a claim, while merely finding that a claim raising these questions was timely filed is sufficient to invoke the quasi-adjudicatory authority of the state agency to resolve factual disputes.

  In *Great Western Power Co. v. Pillsbury*, the California

Supreme Court held that the question whether an employee engaged in willful misconduct went to the basis of the agency's jurisdiction and therefore was open to inquiry by the court. But in *Cardillo v. Liberty Mills Mut. Ins. Co.*, the U.S. Supreme Court refused to disturb administrative findings regarding the geographical coverage of the District of Columbia workers' compensation act.

- The existence of the employer-employee relationship is usually characterized as mixed question of law and fact, and if the facts are not in dispute then the ultimate issue is reviewable. But if the evidence conflicts then the factual issues predominate and the decision by the agency is considered reviewable only under the "not-supported-by-the-evidence" standard. *Wamhoff v. Wagner Electric Co.*, (Mo.). But in the New York decision of *Wittenstein v. Fugazy Continental Corp.*, the existence of the employee-employer relationship was held to be a question of fact, while another New York decision, *O'Rourke v. Long*, characterized it as a mixed question of law and fact. *O'Rourke* held that as a general matter rulings on mixed questions of law and fact are for the agency, not for the courts but then went on to rule that the specific issue in the claim—whether a 10-year-old newspaper carrier was an employee—involved an issue of statutory construction that should have been resolved by the court.
- Whether an injury was in the course of employment is generally regarded as a question of fact. *Cardillo v. Liberty Mills Mut. Ins. Co.* involved complicated facts as to whether the worker was in the course of employment when driving home after work. The employer was required to furnish transportation due to the inaccessibility of the place of work. The U.S. Supreme Court held that the agency's finding that the claimant was in the course of employment when he was injured could not be said as a matter of law to be wrong.
- Date of injury is a question of fact. *Facer v. E.R. Steed Equipment Co.* (Idaho).

• Dependency is a question of fact. *Re Haynes* (Idaho).

Evidence

The rules of evidence are not strictly applied in most workers' compensation agency proceedings. However, in order to support an agency's factual findings, the evidence must be substantial, probative, and relevant; a mere scintilla of evidence is insufficient. A finding based on hearsay evidence may be upheld by a court on review, although there is considerable authority that an order must be based on *some* "legally competent" evidence, i.e., that hearsay evidence alone will not support an award. The cases are split on this issue. The Supreme Judicial Court of Massachusetts has held that hearsay evidence may be the sole basis of a finding *(Stanton's Case)*, but the New York Court of Appeals has held that hearsay evidence alone is insufficient *(Carroll v. Knickerbocker Ice Co.)*. Under Minnesota statutes requiring that agency findings be based on "competent evidence only," the state's supreme court ruled that hearsay evidence could be "competent" within the meaning of the law *(Harrison v. Schafer Constr. Co.)*

Medical-opinion evidence, to be probative in agency proceedings, must conform to the rules applicable generally to such testimony, or a modification of those rules. An expert's opinion evidence must be competent and must be based on personal knowledge or on factual assumptions for which there is a basis in the evidence before the agency. Thus, physicians who examine claimants may render opinions based on the findings of their own medical examination, while a non-examining physician must base any opinion on findings contained in other evidence before the agency or described in medical testimony of an examining physician. A careful analysis of this issue can be found in the Ohio Supreme Court's decision in *Wallace v. Industrial Comm'n*.

TYPES OF REVIEW AVAILABLE

The types of judicial review of final agency decisions are variously labelled, e.g., review or certification of record, writ of mandamus or of error, notice of appeal, petition for hearing, suit to set aside decisions. The procedures to be followed in pursuing review also vary.

Five states—Hawaii, Maryland, Ohio, Vermont, and Washington—permit a review by jury trial of workers' compensation claims. In Maryland's, Ohio's, and Washington's schemes jury trials are *de novo* proceedings, while in Hawaii and Vermont juries review the record developed in the agency proceedings. Jury trials in workers' compensation are similar to other civil trials. The claimant generally has the burden of proof regardless of who prevailed before the agency. *Swift & Co. v. Wreede* (Ohio). The rules of civil and appellate procedure apply in these trials in the same manner as in other civil actions.

In court review of workers' compensation agency decisions, the courts are authorized to take judicial notice of matters of common knowledge. *Lowman v. Amphitheatre School Dist.* (Ariz.). Except as noted above, the burden of proof is on the party attacking the agency's decision. *Moore v. Clark* (Md.).

PROCEDURAL CONSIDERATIONS

Statutes conferring jurisdictions in workers' compensation claims upon courts of general jurisdiction—particularly in those states providing for *de novo* review—are construed strictly. No party has a constitutional right to a jury trial in workers' compensation, nor to a *de novo* review of facts by a court.

Parties to workers' compensation actions are determined by statute. Whether insurance carriers are entitled to be parties before a reviewing court is an open question. In *Transport Ins. Co. v. Jaeger*, the Texas Court of Civil Appeals refused to allow an insurance carrier to amend a petition for review naming the employer rather than itself as plaintiff. This case is a good example both of the strictness with which procedures are followed and of the rule that the parties to an action are limited by the terms of the statute.

The effect of the death of a claimant during the pendency of an appeal in court is also an open question. The majority rule is that the claimant's cause of action survives and may be continued by the claimant's personal representative. The Oklahoma Supreme Court applied this rule in *Western Indem. Co. v. State Indus. Comm'n*. An Ohio court of appeals held the contrary in *Ratliffe v. Flowers*.

Following judicial review, the doctrines of issue preclusion and, where appropriate, claim preclusion apply to the court's decision. The administrative agency is bound by the court's decision, as is any other party. But usually a judicial decision regarding an issue does not mean that the agency has lost jurisdiction over a claim. For example, assume that, in a claim for a spinal injury, the agency decided that the claimant's injury did not aggravate a pre-existing arthritis. Assume further that, on judicial review, a court reversed this finding. (Depending upon the statute, the court could remand the case to the agency to enter an order allowing the additional conditions or it could enter the order of allowance itself and send the claim to the agency for payment.) Notwithstanding the court's reversal of the agency decision, the agency retains its continuing jurisdiction or power to review the claim for new and changed conditions, but the judicial decision is binding on it for the issue of whether the medical condition stems from the injury and is a recognized part of the claim. The Florida appellate decision of *Brevard Bd. of County Comm'r. v. Caldwell* contains a good discussion of the preclusive effect of a judicial decision on an administrative agency.

9

EMPLOYER'S PROTECTIONS AND LIABILITIES

IMMUNITY FROM SUIT

A complying employer cannot be sued for damages for an injury that is covered by workers' compensation. This immunity from suit or exclusivity of the workers' compensation remedy is the benefit that the employer receives under any workers' compensation system.

Under certain circumstances, this immunity may not apply to injuries sustained in the course of and arising out of employment. Possible exceptions to employers' general immunity from lawsuit include the following:

- Injuries not covered by workers' compensation;
- Injuries sustained by an employee of a noncomplying employer;
- Injuries caused by the employer's intentional act;
- Injuries sustained while the employer and employee entered into a separate relationship or "dual capacity" independent of their master/servant relationship;

In addition, an employer may also be liable in a tort or damages action for discharging, demoting, or taking other punitive action in retaliation for employees' filing workers' compensation claims or otherwise pursuing workers' compensation rights.

Injuries Not Covered By Workers' Compensation

The employer's immunity does not extend to those injuries not within the workers' compensation system. This assumption—rather than the exception for the employer's intentional misconduct—is usually used by courts to allow suits by workers against employers based on dignitary torts such as fraud, false imprisonment, and defamation. Two California cases, *Ramey v. General Petroleum Corp.* and *Gates v. Trans Video Corp.* dealt with the issue. *Ramey* held that the workers' compensation act generally does not preclude recovery for such injuries, while *Gates* held the act to be the exclusive remedy for an alleged intentional infliction of emotional distress arising out of employment.

The majority rule is that ordinary common-law remedies such as a suit in negligence for unlimited damages are available to all injuries that are not within the purview of the statutes. The Maine Supreme Court decision in *Niles v. Marine Colloids, Inc.*, for example, held that immunity did not extend to an employer whose alleged negligence resulted in a disease which was not compensable as an occupational disease under state law.

The minority position is that immunity attaches for any injury arising out of and in the course of employment, whether or not compensable. This position has been adopted in Minnesota by decision of its supreme court in *Hyett v. Northwestern Hosp. for Women and Children*, and in Ohio by statute.

Noncomplying Employer

If the employer is noncomplying, then, of course, it has no immunity from suit. Most states provide by statute that an injured worker may elect whether to sue the noncomplying employer at common law for damages or to file a workers' compensation claim. In the common-law action, the employer is deprived of the defenses of fellow-servant rule, contributory negligence, and assumption of risk. The New York case of *People v. Donnelly* contains a discussion of a typical provision. For an example of an atypical provision under which an injured worker could only treat a noncomplying employer as self-insurer and seek penalty and attorney fees, see *Fox v. Stanish* (Ga.).

Intentional Torts

There is a split of authority on the emerging issue of whether an employer's immunity bars suits for work-related injuries that it intentionally inflicts. A significant number of states have not permitted any exception to workers' compensation immunity for intentional torts. The U.S. Court of Appeals for the Tenth Circuit in *Eason v. Frontier Airlines*, for example, found no exception in Colorado law for intentional torts.

The cases may be broken down into three categories: those involving intentional torts, such as assault and battery, for which there is usually a deliberate and knowing intention to harm the employee; those for which the employment relationship has created an affirmative duty on the part of the employer that was violated—the most common of which is failure of an employer to disclose to an employee its knowledge of a dangerous disease or physical condition; and other kinds of intentional or quasi-intentional torts in which the employer exposes an employee to a known hazard.

The semantics of the cases have been subordinated to perceived policy or justice. Hence, the term "intentional" is now capable of shades of meaning and, however counterintuitive it may seem, "deliberate and knowing intent" now means something different from mere "intent," at least in some states. The following discussions of the three categories may illumine this point:

- Deliberate and knowing intent cases, in which the employer actually means to harm an employee are generally recognized as exceptions to employer immunity. These cases often involve physical assaults and common-law tort actions are usually permitted. The New York case of *LePochat v. Pendleton* is a good example of the general rule: An employer who physically attacked his cook was held not immune from suit because (1) the cook's injuries were not accidental and (2) the injuries did not arise out of employment.
- Violation of an affirmative duty is recognized in many states as an exception to employer's immunity. The typical fact pattern—which seems to recur with alarming

uniformity and frequency—is that the employer has failed to disclose that the employee is suffering from a medical condition (usually through exposure at work) which is either correctable at the time that the employer acquires knowledge of it or is at a stage where the progress of the disease could be arrested by removing the worker from the hazardous exposure. The employer typically obtains the knowledge through routine employee physicals.

In many ways abrogation of employer immunity makes *most* sense with this specie of intentional tort. Such conduct by an employer can hardly be described as "in the course of employment." Moreover, the motivation of many employers who withhold such knowledge from diseased employees is a strictly economic consideration of preventing the expense either of a workers' compensation claim or of removing a safety hazard. The powerful economic disincentive of a tort lawsuit presumably could prevent injuries or diseases or deaths of other workers. Finally, these sorts of injuries appear to be quite preventable through such economic disincentives, unlike even the assault and battery cases which might be said to be motivated by heat of passion.

It is some indication of the importance that courts attach to employer's immunity that some states, Indiana *(McLaughlin v. American Oil Co.)* and Texas *(Lotspeich v. Chance Vought Aircraft)*, for example, faced with this fact pattern have refused to permit lawsuit. A slight majority of states that have addressed the issue, however, have recognized the right of the worker to sue the employer under these circumstances—California *(Johns-Manville Products Corp. v. Contra Costa Superior Court)*, New York *(Wojcik v. Aluminum Corp. of America)*, and Ohio *(Delamotte v. Unitcast Div. of Midland Ross Corp.)*.

- Employers who expose workers to known hazards are generally held not to be subject to common-law suit, the usual theories being either that such injuries necessarily are work-related or that the exception for intentional torts should be narrowly construed. The highest courts of two sister states experimented with this exception and were promptly checked by the states' legislatures. The West Virginia Supreme Court ruled that employers were subject to suit if their actions recklessly exposed workers to unnecessary risk, i.e., if they created a "strong probability" that harm would result. (*Mandolidis v. Elkins Indus.*—a decision was effectively overruled by the state's legislature, as stated by the U.S. Court of Appeals for the Fourth Circuit in *Stapleton v. Ashland Oil Co.)* The Ohio Supreme Court ruled similarly in *Blankenship v. Cincinnati Milacron Chemical Co.* and the Ohio legislature responded with a restrictive definition of "intentional tort' and the creation of an intentional tort fund that assesses employers' penalties through the workers' compensation system.

Dual Capacity Doctrine

Under the "dual capacity doctrine," an employer's immunity does not protect it from common-law actions by employees if, in addition to being their employer, the company stands in a second or "dual" capacity that confers obligations unrelated to and independent of those imposed upon it as an employer. Typical cases include alleged medical malpractice in a hospital/employer's emergency-room treatment of an employee, as in the Pennsylvania case of *Tatrai v. Presbyterian Univ. Hosp.*, and a truckdriver injured because of a blowout caused by a defective tire produced by his employer, as in the Ohio appellate case of *Mercer v. Uniroyal, Inc.*

RETALIATION

A growing number of states are permitting employees to sue employers who make adverse employment decisions with regard to them in retaliation for having brought a workers' compensation claim or for having pursued workers' compensation rights. When judicially recognized, this cause of action usually sounds in tort and includes a right to a jury trial for damages. Statutes forbidding retaliatory discharge usually limit the amount of recovery due to the employee and treat the action as a non-jury action in equity. In *Kelsay v. Motorola, Inc.*, the Illinois Supreme Court recognized the new tort of retaliatory discharge but denied punitive damages in that specific case because of the novelty of cause of action. The Missouri appellate decision of *Mitchell v. St. Louis County* bucked the trend altogether and denied any recovery under the retaliation theory.

Federal labor law does not pre-empt state-law claims for retaliatory discharge, even if the discharged employee was covered by a collective-bargaining agreement protecting employees against wrongful discharge. *Lingle v. Norge Div. of Magic Chef* (U.S. Sup. Ct.).

Burdens of proof in retaliatory-discharge cases are evolving along the lines developed in other employment discrimination cases. Thus, the fact that a discharge or adverse employment action comes shortly after the filing of a claim or an attempt to return to work can raise an inference of retaliatory motive. (See *Moore v. McDermott* (La.).) Once the claimant raises the inference of retaliation, the employer may rebut it by showing a legitimate business reason for its decision. (See *Michelson v. Exxon Research and Engineering Co.* (3d Cir.).)

SECOND-INJURY FUNDS

A second-injury fund is an apportionment device for distributing the costs or a part of the costs of a claim against the entire workers' compensation system if the injury or a part of the disability recognized in a claim were caused at least in part by a pre-existing condition. The purpose of second-injury funds is twofold: to encourage the hiring of the physically handicapped and to provide some financial relief to an employer who would otherwise be forced unfairly to bear the entire costs of a claim.

In order to qualify for second-injury relief the employer must establish that it meets the conditions of the statute. This often includes the requirement that the employer had knowledge of the pre-existing condition. Often the pre-existing medical conditions that may form the basis for second-injury fund relief are enumerated by statute. (See the U.S. Chamber of

Commerce Chart, "Second-Injury Funds," Appendix G, for a state-by-state analysis.) Similarly, notice statutes, which require an insurer or employer to notify the second-injury fund of its request to transfer liability for a claim within a certain period of time, are usually strictly construed and mandatory. The Connecticut appellate decision of *Kiernan v. Roadway Express* contains a good discussion of this point.

APPENDIX A
COVERAGE OF LAWS*

* Source: U.S. CHAMBER OF COMMERCE, 1989 ANALYSIS OF WORKERS' COMPENSATION LAWS, "Chart II, Coverage of Laws, January 1, 1989," pp. 5–8.

CHART II — COVERAGE OF LAWS — January 1, 1989

JURISDICTION	EMPLOYMENTS COVERED[1]		EXCEPTIONS[2]	SPECIAL COVERAGE PROVISIONS[1]
	PRIVATE	PUBLIC		
ALABAMA	Compulsory as to employers of 3 or more. Elective as to partners or sole proprietors. Corporate officers may reject.	Compulsory as to all public employments except municipalities of less than 2,000 population. Certain school systems and institutions covered.*	Domestic servants and casual employees	Voluntary for employers of less than 3, including farmers.
ALASKA	Compulsory as to all employments, including elected or appointed corporate executive officers. Effective as to sole proprietors or members of a partnership.	Compulsory as to state and political subdivisions, members of state boards, and commissions. Includes regular firemen if not prohibited by local law. Voluntary as to executive officers of municipal corporations.	Part-time baby sitters, cleaning persons, harvest help, or similar transient help; entertainers employed on contractual basis; and commercial fishermen.	Voluntary as to executive officers of a charitable, religious, educational, or other nonprofit corporation.
AMERICAN SAMOA	Compulsory as to employers of 3 or more; coverage may be required for all hazardous employments.	Compulsory as to all public employments.		Voluntary as to exempt employers.
ARIZONA	Compulsory as to all employments. Elective for working partners. Employee may reject.	Compulsory as to state, counties, cities, towns, municipal corporations, school districts, and volunteers enumerated by statute.	Domestic servants, casual employees, and real estate licensees.	Voluntary as to sole proprietors and employers of domestic servants. Motion picture business employers and employees may be exempted from law provided equal benefits are provided by insurance in domicile state.
ARKANSAS	Compulsory as to employers of 3 or more. Elective as to partners or sole proprietors.	Compulsory as to state agencies, departments, institutions, counties, cities and towns. Excludes workfare recipients.	Farm labor, domestic servants, casual workers, public charities, vendors, or distributors of newspapers and other publications.	Voluntary as to excepted employments. Compulsory for employments in which two or more employees are engaged in building or building repair work; in which one or more employees of a contractor who subcontracts any part of his contract; and in which one or more employees is employed by a subcontractor.
CALIFORNIA	Compulsory as to all employments. Elective for working members of a partnership and for working officers and directors of a private corporation who are sole shareholders.	Compulsory as to all public employments except clerks and deputies serving without remuneration, and to regional occupational centers, programs or school districts offering training to pupils outside attendance area as to enrolled pupils.	Charity workers and volunteer member workers at camps, etc., operated by nonprofit organizations. Employers sponsoring bowling teams. Domestics who work less than 52 hours during preceding 90 days or earn less than $100. Students in sport events (excludes amateur athletic participants who are not employees).	Voluntary as to excepted employments and sponsoring agencies of Economic Opportunity Programs. Employer not liable for injury due to off-duty recreational, social, or athletic activity not part of work-related duties.
COLORADO	Compulsory as to all employments. Corporate officer who is 10% shareholder may reject. Elective as to active employer or partner.	Compulsory as to all salaried public employments. Job trainees deemed employees of training institution.	Employees of religious or charitable organizations, domestic servants and casual employees who earn less than $2,000 per year, volunteer ski lift operators, independent real estate salespersons and brokers, and independent truckers.	All farm labor covered in 1977. Officers of farm corporation may reject coverage.
CONNECTICUT	Compulsory as to all employments. Corporate officer may reject. Elective as to sole proprietors or partners.	Compulsory as to all state, public corporations, and members of General Assembly. Municipalities may elect coverage of elected and appointed officials, police, and firemen.	Casual employees, outworkers,[3] domestics employed less than 26 hours weekly, officers of fraternal organizations paid less than $100 per year.	Voluntary as to excluded employments.
DELAWARE	Compulsory as to all employments. Up to 4 corporate officer-stockholders may reject. Elective as to sole proprietors or partners.	Elective as to state and certain counties, cities, and towns.	Domestic servants; casual employees earning less than $300 in 3 months from one household; farm labor.	Elective as to licensed real estate brokers.

DISTRICT OF COLUMBIA	Compulsory as to all employments.	Separate act is compulsory for all public employments, except officers or employees of the United States, state, or foreign government, and uniformed D.C. police or firemen.	Farm labor, casual employees, master or crew of any vessel, and employees of common carrier by railroad in interstate commerce.	Act applies to employees principally localized in Washington, D.C. Domestic workers covered if employer employs 1 or more for 240 hours or more per quarter.
FLORIDA	Compulsory as to employers of 3 or more. Elective as to corporate officers, partners, and sole proprietors.	Compulsory as to state and political subdivisions (includes volunteers), except elected officials.	Domestic servants, casual employees, 12 or fewer casual or 5 or fewer regular farm labor, professional athletes, employees of common carriers, and volunteers (except for government entities).	Voluntary as to excepted employments. Excludes real estate salesmen, solely on commission. Numerical exemption inapplicable to employees of subcontractors.
GEORGIA	Compulsory as to all employers of 3 or more. Elective as to active partners or sole proprietors.	Compulsory as to state, county, municipal corporations, and political subdivisions including school districts. Voluntary as to planning commissions.	Farm labor, domestic servants, employees of common carriers by railroad, casual labor and licensed real estate salesmen and brokers.	Voluntary as to excepted employments.
GUAM	Compulsory as to all industrial employments.*	Compulsory as to paid and voluntary work done for Government of Guam or any political subdivision.	Casual labor and members of Territorial Board of Education.	All contracts of hire in the Territory for work outside the Territory are presumed to allow remedies under the Guam Workers' Compensation Law.
HAWAII	Compulsory as to all industrial employments.*	Compulsory as to all public officials, elective or appointed. Covers public board members.	Volunteers of religious, charitable, or nonprofit organizations. Domestics who earn less than $225 during each quarter in the preceding year. Unpaid corporate officers with 25% + shares of corporation with no employees.	Voluntary as to employments not defined as industrial.
IDAHO	Compulsory as to all employments. Elective as to corporate officers who are 10% shareholders, sole proprietors, and working members of partnership.	Compulsory as to all public employments except officials at secondary school athletic contests.	Agricultural pursuits, domestic servants, casual labor, indwelling members of employer's family, outworkers,[3] employment not for money, airmen, and commission real estate salesmen and brokers.	Employees within state who work for employers domiciled in another state are covered. Credit is provided for benefits paid to employees under the law of other states.
ILLINOIS	Compulsory as to enumerated "extra hazardous" employments (including occupational diseases). Elective as to partners and sole proprietors.	Compulsory as to all public employments except members of fire and police departments in cities over 200,000 population (such firemen covered to extent of burn-related disfigurement).*	Certain farm labor, domestics, and persons not in usual course of employer's business; real estate brokers and salesmen paid by commission only.	Voluntary as to excluded employments.** Corporate officers of small business may reject.
INDIANA	Compulsory as to all employments including corporate officers. Elective as to sole proprietors, or partners.	Compulsory as to state, municipal corporations, and political subdivisions; includes state legislators, and elected and appointed officials.	Farm labor, domestic servants, casual workers, and railroad workers, and licensed real estate professionals.*	Compulsory as to coal mining and for students in cooperative education.
IOWA	Compulsory as to all employments but up to 4 corporate officers may reject. Elective for proprietors and working partners.	Compulsory as to all public employments, except firemen and policemen entitled to pension fund. Covers highway safety patrol officers, conservation officers, and agricultural workers at state universities.	Domestic and casual workers earning under $200 per quarter; farm labor, if employer payroll under $2,500 per year.	Voluntary as to excepted employments. Persons receiving employment training or evaluations in an approved facility are covered for PP or PT disabilities. Under certain conditions, truck owner-operators are considered independent contractors and are required to maintain own WC coverage.

NOTE: State courts vary in decisions whether minimum of persons must be in state.

[1]Compensation laws are classified as compulsory or elective. A compulsory law requires every employer to accept the act and pay the compensation specified. An elective act is one in which the employer has the option of either accepting or rejecting the act, but if he rejects it he loses the customary common law defenses (risk assumed by employee, negligence of fellow servants, and contributory negligence). In most states workers in excepted or excluded employments may be brought under coverage of the act through voluntary action of the employer. In other states, such action of the employer must be concurred in by the employees.

[2]Applying to private employments only. The exceptions for public employments are given under "Employments Covered—Public."

[3]Outworker is person to whom articles are given for cleaning, repair, etc., at home.

Ala. *Employees of all county and city bds. of education, Ala. Inst. for Deaf and Blind, and 2-yr. colleges under state bd. of educ. control. Special act covers employees of U.S.S. Alabama Battleship Comm. and authorizes excess medical care benefits not to exceed $10,000 per employee, also, for employees of Department of Agriculture and Industries. Special act covers employees of Tannehill Furnace and Foundry Commission.

Guam *Employment in trade, occupation, or profession, carried on by employer for pecuniary gain.

Hawaii *Employment in trade, occupation, or profession, carried on by employer for pecuniary gain.

Ill. *Townships may elect coverage for participants in job training or work program.
**The law is "elective" as to private employments of a nonhazardous nature, but it does not abrogate the employer's defenses if he does not accept the act, and thus is considered to be voluntary.

Ind. *Elective for officer of a charitable, religious, educational, or nonprofit corporation.

CHART II □ COVERAGE OF LAWS □ January 1, 1989 (continued)

JURISDICTION	EMPLOYMENTS COVERED[1] PRIVATE	EMPLOYMENTS COVERED[1] PUBLIC	EXCEPTIONS[2]	SPECIAL COVERAGE PROVISIONS[1]
KANSAS	Compulsory as to all employments, including corporate executive officers. Elective as to partners, individuals, or self-employeds.	Compulsory as to all public employments. Members of firemen's relief associations may elect to accept or reject coverage. Public agencies or entities may elect coverage for persons required to perform community service work.	Farm labor or any employer whose gross annual payroll is not more than $10,000; real estate brokers and salespersons on commission.	Compulsory as to eleemosynary institutions. Voluntary as to excluded employments. Labor unions and associations may elect coverage for their members who perform services and are not full-time employees.
KENTUCKY	Compulsory as to all employments, including corporate executives. Elective as to owner of business or partner. Worker may reject voluntarily prior to injury.	Compulsory as to state and political subdivisions, including elected and appointed state officials and employees of the General Assembly.	Domestic servants if employer employs fewer than 2 each regularly employed 40 hours a week; casual workers employed less than 20 consecutive days; agricultural labor; worker for charitable or religious organization in return for aid or sustenance; and participant in carpool to and from work.	Specifically covers newsboys, operators of coal mines and members of volunteer ambulance service. Voluntary as to excluded employments.
LOUISIANA	Compulsory as to all employments, including corporate executives. Corporate officers who are 10% shareholders and sole proprietors may reject.	Compulsory as to all public employments, except sheriffs' deputies and officials. Subdivisions may cover elective and appointive officials.	Crews of crop spraying aircraft while acting as contractors, or employees of persons principally engaged in agriculture; real estate brokers and salesmen; domestic workers.	Excludes officers of nonprofit charitable, fraternal, cultural, or religious corporations or associations.
MAINE	Compulsory as to all employments, including corporate executive officers. Corporate officers who are 20% shareholders may reject. Elective as to self-employed persons or partners.	Compulsory as to state, counties, cities, towns, and quasi-municipal corporations. Includes firemen and police and volunteer firemen and emergency medical services personnel.	Domestic workers, seasonal or casual agricultural or aquacultural employees.* Maritime employee in interstate or foreign commerce, or lobster sternman. Commission-paid real estate salesman or broker.** Independent contractor. Employee harvesting 150 cords of wood from farm wood lot. Voluntary participant in employer-sponsored athletic event. Elected or appointed executive officers of a charitable, religious, educational or other nonprofit corporation.***	Voluntary as to excluded employments. Parent, spouse, or child of sole proprietor, partner, or corporate officer who is a 20% shareholder, may reject coverage.
MARYLAND	Compulsory as to all employments, including corporate officers. Elective as to partners or sole proprietors. Corporate farm officers who are 20% shareholders may reject. Elective for officers owning 20% or more of a professional services corporation and performing professional services for that corporation.	Compulsory as to state, counties, cities, and their agencies; paid firemen in certain counties; prisoners working for county roads boards; forest wardens; crewmen and fire fighters for Department of Forest and Parks, jurors for non-federal courts.	Domestic workers who earn less than $250 in a quarter from a single household; certain maintenance workers, not employed for 30 consecutive days around a private home; seasonal, migratory farm labor within 25 miles of residence who work no more than 13 weeks a year and who do not operate machinery or equipment, and commission-paid real estate salesman or broker.	Voluntary as to excluded employments. Officers of close corporation may reject. Small employers of farm labor may be insured under a group policy.
MASSACHUSETTS	Compulsory as to all employments.	Compulsory as to state; elective as to counties, cities, and districts having power of taxation. Municipalities required to indemnify police and firemen. Cities and towns may cover certain elected or appointed officials.	Seasonal and casual labor, domestic servants employed less than 16 hours a week, masters and seamen in interstate commerce covered by federal law, athletes whose contracts provide wages during job disability, commission-paid salespersons, independent taxi drivers, and voluntary participants in recreational activities.	Voluntary as to domestic servants hired casually or on a seasonal basis.
MICHIGAN	Compulsory as to all employers of 3 or more, or less than 3 if 1 is employed for 35 hours per week for 13 weeks by same employer.*	Compulsory as to all public employments, including Michigan Conservation Corps members. Trainees in federally funded training program deemed employees of sponsoring public entity.	Professional athletes whose average weekly wage is more than 200% of statewide average weekly wage; domestic servants who work less than 35 hours a week for 13 weeks a year; licensed real-estate salesmen.	Voluntary as to employer of 2 or less, and domestic service. Family members may be excluded by endorsement.

MINNESOTA	Compulsory to most employments. Elective as to partners or officers of certain family farms or close corporations and their families.	Compulsory as to most public employments. Subdivisions may cover elective and appointed officers.	Certain casual labor; household workers who earn under $1,000 per 3 months from one private household, family farms with annual farm labor payroll under $8,000, railroad workers covered by federal law, and nonprofit corporations with annual payroll under $1,000; commercial thresher or baler for family farm.*	Election must be in writing. Person, partnership or corporation may elect coverage for independent contractors for a fee.
MISSISSIPPI	Compulsory as to all employers of 5 or more. Corporate officers may reject.	Compulsory as to all public employments, including political subdivisions of the state. Specifically excludes handicapped in state sheltered workshop programs.	Domestic servants; farmers; farm labor; newspaper distributors; officers of nonprofit charitable, fraternal, cultural, or religious corporations or associations.	Voluntary as to exempted employers.
MISSOURI	Compulsory as to all employers of 5 or more.* Elective for partners and sole proprietors.	Compulsory as to all public employments, including elected and appointed state officials, contractors of a public corporation, state militia, and sheriffs and deputy sheriffs. Compulsory for workers on state welfare projects under federal Economic Opportunity Act.	Farm labor, domestic servants, occasional labor for private household, qualified real estate agents, members of employer's family by marriage or consanguinity, inmates confined to a state prison, penitentiary, county or municipal jail, residents of mental health facilities and unpaid volunteers of a tax-exempt organization.	Voluntary as to exempt employments, employers of less than 5 employees, and salaried officers of Missouri farm corporations.
MONTANA	Compulsory as to all employments. Corporate officers may reject. Elective as to partners and sole proprietors.	Compulsory as to all public employments, including public contractors, and volunteer rescue workers.	Domestic and casual employment, employers covered by federal law, person performing services for aid and sustenance only, officials at amateur athletic events, real estate broker or salesman, direct sellers of consumer goods, and newspaper carriers or free-lance correspondents. Cosmetologists and barbers who qualify as independent contractors may exempt themselves.	Coverage is mandatory for partner or sole proprietor who is independent contractor (except real estate or farm services), but may apply for personal exemption. Voluntary as to exempt employments.
NEBRASKA	Compulsory as to all employments. Corporate officers who are 25% shareholders may reject. Elective as to proprietors, partners or self-employed.	Compulsory as to all employments, including officials elected or appointed for fixed terms.	Farm labor and domestic servants	Voluntary as to farm labor and domestic service.
NEVADA	Compulsory as to all employments. Elective as to sole proprietors.	Compulsory as to all employments, including public contractors. Also includes unpaid members of state departments, boards, commissions, agencies, or bureaus appointed by a statutory authority; members of local bands and orchestras.	Farm labor; domestic servants; casual employees; employees engaged without pay in employer's social or athletic events; voluntary ski patrolmen; and any clergyman, rabbi or lay reader.	Voluntary as to exempt employments. Employee may elect compensation if mandated employer is uninsured.
NEW HAMPSHIRE	Compulsory as to all employments. First 3 corporate officers not counted as employees.* Elective as to partners and sole proprietors.	Compulsory as to all public employments.	Railroad workers covered under F.E.L.A. (Jones Act).	
NEW JERSEY	Elective as to all employments.	Compulsory as to all public employments.	Casual workers, maritime workers, and railroad workers engaged in interstate commerce.	
NEW MEXICO	Compulsory as to employers of 3 or more. Corporate officers who are 10% shareholders may reject. Elective as to partner or self-employed.	Compulsory as to state; counties; cities; towns; schools, drainage, irrigation, or conservancy districts; public instruction or administrative boards; includes elected or appointed officials.	Farm or ranch labor, domestic servants, casual employees, and real estate salespersons.	Voluntary as to farm labor, domestic service, and where less than 3 are employed. Compulsory for charitable organizations employing workers.

NOTE: State courts vary in decisions whether minimum number of persons must be in state.

[1]Compensation laws are classified as compulsory or elective. A compulsory law requires every employer to accept the act and pay the compensation specified. An elective act is one in which the employer has the option of either accepting or rejecting the act, but if he rejects it he loses the customary common law defenses (risk assumed by employee, negligence of fellow servants, and contributory negligence). In most states workers in excepted or excluded employments may be brought under coverage of the act through voluntary action of the employer. In other states, such action of the employer must be concurred in by the employees.

[2]Applying to private employments only. The exceptions for public employments are given under "Employments Covered—Public."

Me. *Employers of six or fewer agricultural or aquacultural employees exempt if employer maintains liability insurance policy with limits of not less than $100,000 per employee and medical coverage of not less than $1,000.
**Provided that broker or salesman is independent contractor and signs contract with agency indicating such.
***No compensation allowed if injury or death of employee is brought about by willful intention of himself or another, or by intoxication while on duty.

Mich. *Corporate officer who is 10% shareholder of corporation with up to 10 shareholders may reject.

Minn. *Act does not apply to persons covered by Domestic Volunteer Service Act of 1973, as amended.

Mo. *Employers who do not elect coverage are liable to suit with defenses abrogated.

N.H. *If corporation adds fourth officer or has any other employees, all must be covered, including the first three.

CHART II ☐ COVERAGE OF LAWS ☐ January 1, 1989 (continued)

JURISDICTION	EMPLOYMENTS COVERED[1]		EXCEPTIONS[2]	SPECIAL COVERAGE PROVISIONS[1]
	PRIVATE	PUBLIC		
NEW YORK	Compulsory as to all employments. Elective as to partners, self-employed, sole shareholder/officer and two shareholders/officers.*	Compulsory as to state and subdivisions when worker is engaged in hazardous occupations enumerated. Covers school aides and public school teachers in districts outside New York City. Voluntary as to municipal corporations in nonhazardous employments.	Farm labor if payroll during prior year was less than $1,200; volunteer workers; domestic worker not employed by same employer at least 40 hours per week; teacher or nonmanual laborer for religious, charitable, or educational institution; certain real estate salespersons, corporate officer who is sole shareholder and has no other employees; babysitters, and casual employment or repairs in or about a one-family owner occupied residence.	Voluntary as to exempt employments and for certain employment in fulfillment of probationary sentence.
NORTH CAROLINA	Compulsory as to all employers of 3 or more and all employments with exposure to radiation. Corporate officers count toward total number of employees but may reject. Elective as to partner or sole proprietor.	Compulsory as to public employments, public and quasi-public corporations, and elective officials.	Farm labor, domestic servants, casual workers, railroad workers, voluntary ski patrolmen, individual sawmill or logging operators with fewer than 10 employees who operate less than 60 days over a 6-month period.	Voluntary as to casual employees, domestic servants, and employers of fewer than 3 employees. Compulsory as to agricultural employer with 10 or more full-time nonseasonal workers.
NORTH DAKOTA	Compulsory as to all hazardous employments. Elective as to corporate officers, partners or sole proprietors, and resident family members.	Compulsory as to all public employments.	Farm labor, domestic servants, casual workers, illegal enterprises or occupations, and clergy.	Voluntary as to nonhazardous and excluded employments.
OHIO	Compulsory as to all employments. Elective as to partners and sole proprietors.	Compulsory as to state, counties, cities, townships, incorporated villages, and school districts.	Casual and domestic workers paid less than $160 by one employer in any 3-month period.	Elective as to officers of family farm corporations and for ordained or licensed ministers in the exercise of their ministry.
OKLAHOMA	Compulsory as to all employments. Elective as to 10% shareholders, partners, sole proprietors, and owner-operator truckers.	Compulsory as to the state, counties, cities, or municipalities except where equivalent schemes are in force.	Domestic and casual employees of homeowner whose annual payroll is under $10,000, worker covered by federal law, agricultural/horticultural employer whose annual payroll is under $100,000; real estate salesmen and brokers.	Excludes certain persons sentenced to public service, assigned to work release or private prison industry programs.
OREGON	Compulsory as to all employments. Elective as to sole proprietors, partners, and corporate officers who are also directors with a substantial ownership interest.*	Compulsory as to state, departments, cities, or towns and other political subdivisions. Covers volunteer trainees in state schools for deaf and blind. Excludes cities under 200,000 population with equivalent compensation.	Domestics, casual labor, interstate transportation, certain charitable or relief work, newspaper carriers, certain amateur athletes and sports officials, volunteer ski patrols and volunteers in the ACTION Program, certain personnel under federal permits, owners and operators of certain motor vehicles, and commission-paid real estate agents.	Voluntary as to excepted employments. Covers clients in Vocational Rehabilitation Division. Owner-operator of equipment for hire or taxi may elect coverage. Any employer may elect coverage for nonsubject workers.
PENNSYLVANIA	Compulsory as to all employments.	Compulsory as to all public employments except elected officials. Students in vocational work program covered as employees of employer.	Domestic or casual labor, outworker[3], farmer with 1 employee who works less than 20 days a year or earns less than $150 a year.	Voluntary as to casual and domestic service.*
PUERTO RICO	Compulsory as to all employments.	Compulsory as to all salaried public employments.	Casual and domiciliary workers.	Voluntary for sole proprietors and their families when supervising or engaging in manual labor in their business or farm.
RHODE ISLAND	Compulsory as to all employers of 4 or more, and employers in hazardous occupations.	Compulsory as to the state and city of Providence; elective as to cities or towns.	Agriculture, domestic service. Excludes van pooling recipients except driver.	Voluntary as to agriculture, domestic service, and employers or less than 4 employees, except those in hazardous occupations. Excludes employer-sponsored social or athletic activity.
SOUTH CAROLINA	Elective as to all employers of 4 or more, including active partners and sole proprietors whose employees are eligible for benefits.	Compulsory as to all public employments* except elective and appointive officials. Coverage extended to members of the State and National Guard.	Casual employees, persons engaged in selling agricultural products, farm labor, railroads, express companies, state and county fair associations, employer with annual payroll under $3,000.	Voluntary as to excluded employments.

SOUTH DAKOTA	Compulsory as to all employments. Elective as to employer performing labor incidental to job.	Compulsory as to all public employments, except elected or appointed officials. Firemen covered. Subdivisions of state may elect to cover elected and appointed officials. Students in vocational work program covered as employees of employer.	Farm labor; domestic servants if employed more than 20 hours in any week and more than 6 weeks in any 13-week period; and workfare participants.	Voluntary as to farm labor and domestic service. Compulsory as to operators of farm machinery, e.g., threshers, combines, shellers, cornhuskers.
TENNESSEE	Compulsory as to all employers of 5 or more. Corporate officers may reject. Elective as to partners and sole proprietors.	Voluntary as to state and political subdivisions.	Farm labor, domestic servants, casual employees, employees of interstate common carriers, and voluntary ski patrolmen.	Voluntary as to employers of less than 5.
TEXAS	Elective as to all employments. Elective as to corporate officers, partners, and sole proprietors. Farm/ranch operator may elect to cover self, partner, corporate officer or family member.	State provides self-insurance coverage for Highway Dept., University of Texas, Texas A&M University, and all other state employees. Counties, municipalities, and other political subdivisions may provide compensation for their employees.*	Domestic servants, railways used as common carriers, and employees not in usual course of employer's business; seasonal farm/ranch labor for employer with payroll under $25,000,** and other farm/ranch labor for employer with payroll under $75,000.***	Specifically covers motorbus companies. Elective as to excepted workers. Real estate salesmen by commission only may elect coverage.
UTAH	Compulsory as to all employments. Elective as to partners and sole proprietors.	Compulsory as to all public employments, including community service workers and volunteers.*	Casual employees. Farm employers whose payroll is less than $2,500 per year; who do not employ 4 persons for 40 hours per week for 13 weeks during year; or employer-owner's family. Domestics who work less than 40 hours per week for a single employer. Real estate salesman or broker.	Voluntary as to farm labor and domestic service.
VERMONT	Compulsory as to all employments. Corporate officers may reject. Elective as to sole proprietors and partners.	Compulsory as to all public employees, including legislators while in session, teachers, police, firemen, town and school employees, other municipal employees entitled to pensions, and road commissioners or selectmen engaged in highway maintenance or construction.*	Casual or domestic employees; amateur athletes; farm labor where employer's payroll is under $2,000 per year.	Specifically covers circuses and carnivals. Exempted farmers and employers of domestics may elect coverage.
VIRGIN ISLANDS	Compulsory as to all employments. Elective as to partners and sole proprietors.	Compulsory as to all public employments.	Casual and domestic employees, and volunteers for charitable organizations	Voluntary as to exempt employers and employees.
VIRGINIA	Compulsory as to employers of 3 or more and farm employer with more than 2 full-time employees. Elective for partners and sole proprietors. Corporate officers may reject for accidental injury only.	Compulsory as to all public employments, except administrative officers and employees elected or appointed for definite terms.* Includes judges of Supreme Court and Circuit Court and judges and clerks of juvenile, domestic relations, and district courts.	Casual employees; horticultural and farm laborers; domestic servants; employees of steam railroads; employments not in usual course of employer's trade, business, or occupation; and real estate salesmen/associated brokers on commission, under independent contract, or who are not treated as employees for federal income tax purposes.	Voluntary as to employers of less than 3, farm labor, and domestics.

NOTE: State courts vary in decisions whether minimum number of persons must be in state.

[1]Compensation laws are classified as compulsory or elective. A compulsory law requires every employer to accept the act and pay the compensation specified. An elective act is one in which the employer has the option to either accept or reject the act, but if he rejects it he loses the customary common law defenses (risk assumed by employee, negligence of fellow servants, and contributory negligence). In most states workers in excepted or excluded employments may be brought under coverage of the act through voluntary action of the employer. In other states, such action of the employer must be concurred in by the employees.

[2]Applying to private employments only. The exceptions for public employments are given under "Employments Covered—Public."

[3]Outworker is person to whom articles are given for cleaning, repair, etc., at home.

N.Y. *Elective as to unsalaried executive officer of not-for-profit unincorporated association or corporation, and as to executive officer of religious, charitable or educational corporation or veterans' organization.

Ore. *Ownership interest not required for certain family farms.

Pa. *Elective for members of certain State Treasurer, and State religious sects whose tenets prohibit benefits from insurance, provided the sect makes provision for its members.

*S.C. Department of Parole and Community Corrections may elect coverage for convicted persons performing community service or participating in a work program.

Texas *Subdivisions may elect to cover officer deemed volunteer firemen, police, and emergency medical personnel.
**To be adjusted for inflation.
***$50,000 for 1988-90, $25,000 or 3 more employees for 1991 (dollar amounts to be adjusted for inflation).

Utah *Volunteers are eligible only for workers' compensation medical benefits, not indemnity benefits.

Vt. *Municipalities may elect coverage of other employees. Excludes other elected officials, certain judges, sheriffs, and county treasurers and clerks.

Va. *Governing body of county, city, or town may elect coverage of its members.

CHART II □ COVERAGE OF LAWS □ January 1, 1989 (continued)

JURISDICTION	EMPLOYMENTS COVERED[1]		EXCEPTIONS[2]	SPECIAL COVERAGE PROVISIONS[1]
	PRIVATE	PUBLIC		
WASHINGTON	Compulsory as to all employments. Elective as to partners, sole proprietors, joint venturers, and corporate officers who are shareholders/directors.	Compulsory as to all public employments.	Home repair and gardening workers, railroad workers, unpaid workers in eleemosynary institutions, children under 18 on a family farm, jockeys, and employments not in usual course of employer's business.	Covers apprentices registered with Apprenticeship Council. Excludes purchaser of contract musical or entertainment performance.
WEST VIRGINIA	Compulsory as to all employments. Elective as to partners, sole proprietors, and officers of associations and corporations.	Compulsory as to all public employments, including elected officials. Elective for churches.	Domestic workers, farm labor of 5 or fewer, casual employers, and employees working out of state (except temporarily).	Elective as to employers in organized professional sports, including thoroughbred horse racing.
WISCONSIN	Compulsory as to all employments (except farm labor) if payroll is $500 or more in any calendar quarter for services in the state. Compulsory as to farmers with 6 or more employees.	Compulsory as to all employees, including state legislators. Includes certain vocational education students.	Domestic servants and casual employees.	Voluntary as to excluded employments. Elective as to working sole proprietors and partners. Elective for up to two officers of a closely held corporation. Includes participants in community work experience program.
WYOMING	Compulsory as to enumerated "extra-hazardous" occupations conducted for gain. Elective as to corporate officers.*	Compulsory as to state, counties, and muncipal corporations when engaged in "extrahazardous" work.	Casual employees, office workers, sales clerks, farm and ranch workers, and independent contractors.	Elective as to farm and ranch workers and non-extra hazardous occupations if employer elects coverage (except dude ranches).
F.E.C.A.		All civil employees of the U.S. government, including wholly owned instrumentalities, and persons performing activities of civil employees without pay.		
LONGSHORE ACT	Compulsory as to all maritime employment nationwide, including longshoring, harborworking, shipbuilding, or ship repair.	Officers and employees of the U.S. or any state or foreign governments are not covered.	Master or crew of any vessel and persons unloading or repairing vessels of less than 18 tons.* Not applicable to maritime employment in Puerto Rico.**	Act also applies to workers at military bases and public works abroad; welfare and morale service workers for military abroad; and workers for nonappropriated funds (ship's services, PX's, etc.) in U.S. and abroad.

[1]Compensation laws are classified as compulsory or elective. A compulsory law requires every employer to accept the act and pay the compensation specified. An elective act is one in which the employer has the option of either accepting or rejecting the act, but if he rejects it he loses the customary common law defenses (risk assumed by employee, negligence of fellow servants, and contributory negligence). In most jurisdictions workers in excepted or excluded employments may be brought under coverage of the act through voluntary action of the employer. In other jurisdictions, such action of the employer must be concurred in by the employees.

[2]Applying to private employments only. The exceptions for public employments are given under "Employments Covered—Public."

[3]Outworker is person to whom articles are given for cleaning, repair, etc., at home.

Wyo. *Salary of corporate officer is $2,400 minimum, $4,800 maximum.

Longshore *Also excluded to extent covered by state law are: office, clerical, secretarial, security or data processing employees; club, camp, recreational operation, restaurant, museum or retail outlet employees; marina employees not engaged in construction, replacement or expansion; persons temporarily on premises not doing work normally performed by employer; aquaculture workers; builders, repairers or dismantlers of recreational vessels under 65 feet in length; and master or crew member of any vessel.

**By decisional law. Garcia v. Friesecke, 597 F.2d 284 (1st Cir.), *cert. denied* 444 U.S. 940 (1979).

APPENDIX B
Coverage of Occupational Diseases*

* Source: U.S. Chamber of Commerce, 1989 Analysis of Workers' Compensation Laws, "Chart IV, Coverage of Occupational Diseases, January 1, 1989," pp. 10–14.

CHART IV COVERAGE OF OCCUPATIONAL DISEASES January 1, 1989

JURISDICTION	NATURE OF COVERAGE[1]	MEDICAL BOARDS	ONSET OF DISABILITY OR DEATH	TIME LIMIT ON CLAIM FILING	DEDUCTIONS FROM DEATH AWARDS	MEDICAL CARE	COMPENSATION[2]
ALABAMA	All diseases		Death—within 3 years after last exposure or last payment. Radiation or occupational pneumoconiosis*—exposure must occur in at least 12 months over 5 years prior to last exposure.	Disability—within 2 years after last exposure or last payment (radiation—within 2 years and claimant knows/should know relation to employment). Death—within 2 years after death or last payment. Coalminer's pneumoconiosis—within 3 years after total disability or death and claimant knows/should know relation to employment.		Unlimited	Same as for accidents. Coalminer's pneumoconiosis—total disability or death compensated same as Federal Black Lung Act.
ALASKA	All diseases			2 years after knowledge of relation to employment. Within 1 year after death.		Unlimited	Same as for accidents
AMERICAN SAMOA	All diseases	Claimant examined by physician selected by Commissioner.		Within 1 year after claimant knows/should know relation to employment.		Unlimited	Same as for accidents
ARIZONA	All diseases	Board of 3 medical consultants may be appointed by Commission. Report is prima facie evidence of facts.	Silicosis or asbestosis—employer liable only if exposure during 2 years.	Within 1 year after disability or accrual of right; excusable.*	Disability payments	Unlimited	Same as for accidents
ARKANSAS	All diseases		Disability or death—within 1 year after last exposure (3 years for silicosis or asbestosis), or 7 years for death following continuous disability.* Does not apply to radiation. Silicosis or asbestosis presumed nonoccupational absent exposure in 5 years over 10 years prior to disability (2 of 5 years in-state unless same employer).	Disability—within 2 years after last exposure (silicosis or asbestosis—within 1 year from disablement; radiation—within 2 years from diagnosis). Death—within 2 years.		Unlimited	Same as for accidents. Silicosis and asbestosis—partial disability less than 33-1/3% noncompensable.*
CALIFORNIA	All diseases.			Disability—within 1 year from injury or last payment. Death—within 1 year after death (for death within 1 year after injury); 1 year after last medical payment; or 1 year after death if compensation paid; no proceedings more than 240 weeks after injury except for claims based on asbestos exposure.*		Unlimited	Same as for accidents
COLORADO	All diseases*	Committee of 3 physicians reviews care or services for necessity and appropriateness, on request of a party.	Disability—within 5 years after injury (no limit for radiation, asbestosis, silicosis, or anthracosis). Silicosis or asbestosis—employer liable only if exposure lasts 60 days.	Within 3 years after disability or death (5 years in case of ionizing radiation, asbestosis, silicosis, or anthracosis or if reasonable excuse).		Unlimited	Same as for accidents

CONNECTICUT	All diseases	Panel of 3 physicians may be appointed by Commissioner to resolve medical issues involving lung disease.		Within 3 years after first manifestation of disease (within 2 years if death occurs within 2 years after first manifestation of disease, or 1 year after death, whichever is later).		Unlimited	Same as for accidents
DELAWARE	All diseases			Disability or death—within 1 year after claimant knows relation to employment.		Unlimited	Same as for accidents
DISTRICT OF COLUMBIA	All diseases			Within 1 year after injury, death, last payment, or knowledge of relation to employment.		Unlimited	Same as for accidents
FLORIDA	All diseases		Death—following continuous disability and within 350 weeks after last exposure. Employer liable for dust disease only if exposure lasts 60 days.	Within 2 years after disablement, death, or last payment.		Unlimited	Same as for accidents
GEORGIA	All diseases	Independent medical exam by physician chosen by agreement of parties or appointment of the Board.	Within one year of date when employee knew or should have known of existence of an occupational disease but in no event more than seven (7) years after last injurious exposure.	Within one year of date when employee knew or should have known of existence of an occupational disease but in no event more than seven (7) years after last injurious exposure.	Disability payments	Unlimited	Same as for accidents
GUAM	All diseases			Within 1 year after injury, death, or last payment.		Unlimited	Same as for accidents
HAWAII	All diseases			Within 2 years after claimant knows relation to employment.		Unlimited	Same as for accidents

[1]Employer and insurance carrier at time of last exposure are liable in Arkansas, Colorado, Florida, Georgia, Illinois, Indiana, Kansas, Kentucky, Maine, Maryland, Minnesota, New Hampshire, North Carolina, Oklahoma, Tennessee, Vermont, and Virginia. The employer at time of last exposure is liable in Alabama, Arizona, Iowa, Michigan, Missouri, Montana, New Mexico, Pennsylvania, South Dakota, Texas, and Utah. Liability is apportioned among responsible employers in New York and Rhode Island. California limits liability to employer during last year of exposure.

[2]Benefits determined as of the date of last exposure or last injurious exposure in Arkansas, Georgia, Illinois, Indiana, Kentucky, Louisiana, Maine, Michigan, Minnesota, Missouri, New Jersey, South Dakota, Texas, Washington, Wisconsin, and Wyoming. Benefits determined as of the date of disability, knowledge, or manifestation in Alabama, Alaska, Arizona, California, Colorado, Connecticut, Delaware, Florida, Hawaii, Idaho, Iowa, Maryland, Massachusetts, Mississippi, Montana, Nebraska, New Hampshire, New Mexico, New York, North Carolina, North Dakota, Ohio, Oklahoma, Oregon, Pennsylvania, Rhode Island, South Carolina, Tennessee, Utah, Vermont, and West Virginia.

Ala. *Radiation illness caused by gradual exposure.

Ariz. *Limit on filing runs from when injury is manifest or when claimant knows/should know relation to employment; tolled during incapacity.

Ark. *Silicosis or asbestosis—worker who is affected but not disabled may leave work and receive up to 26 weeks of benefits plus up to $400 for retraining.

Calif. *Date of injury is date of disability and claimant knows/should know relation to employment.

Colo. *Supreme Court held that employees may be entitled to benefits for job-related mental or emotional stress. *City of Boulder v. Streeb, 706 P.2d 786 (1985).*

Ga. *Byssinosis claims diagnosed before July 1, 1983, must be filed before July 1, 1984.

**Year is 200 days exposure over 12 months.

CHART IV ☐ COVERAGE OF OCCUPATIONAL DISEASES ☐ January 1, 1989 (continued)

JURISDICTION	NATURE OF COVERAGE[1]	MEDICAL BOARDS	ONSET OF DISABILITY OR DEATH	TIME LIMIT ON CLAIM FILING	DEDUCTIONS FROM DEATH AWARDS	MEDICAL CARE	COMPENSATION[2]
IDAHO	All diseases		Within 1 year after last exposure (4 years for silicosis, 7 years for death following continuous disability). Employer liable for nonacute disease only if exposure lasts 60 days. Silicosis—exposure must occur in 5 years during 10 years prior to disablement (last 2 in-state unless same employer).	Within 1 year after manifestation or death. Silicosis—within 4 years after last exposure. Radiation or unusual disease—within 1 year after incapacity, disability, or death and claimant knows/should know relation to employment.	Disability payments	Unlimited	Same as for accidents. Silicosis—partial disability noncompensable*
ILLINOIS	All diseases		Disability—within 2 years after last exposure (3 years for berylliosis or silicosis, 25 years for asbestosis or radiation).	Disability—within 3 years after disablement or 2 years after last payment. Death—within 3 years after death or last payment. Coal-miner's pneumoconiosis—within 5 years after last exposure or last payment. Radiation or asbestosis—within 25 years after last exposure.	Disability payments but with minimum compensation	Unlimited	Same as for accidents
INDIANA	All diseases		Disablement—within 2 years after last exposure (3 years if caused by coal or silica dust, 35 years if caused by asbestos*); radiation—within 2 years after claimant knows/should know relation to employment. Death—within 2 years after disablement or during pendency of disability claim filed within that period; within 2 years after fixed disability expires but no later than 300 weeks after disablement. Employer liable for silicosis or asbestosis only if exposure lasts 60 days.	Within 2 years after disablement or death.	Disability payments	Unlimited	Same as for accidents
IOWA	All diseases	Medical Board may decide controverted medical questions or provide medical examinations for certain employees.	Disability or death—within 1 year after last exposure (3 years for pneumoconiosis; 7 years for death following continuous disability). Pneumoconiosis presumed nonoccupational absent exposure in 5 years over 10 years prior to disability (2 of 5 years in-state).	Within 2 years after death or disablement or 3 years after last payment.* Radiation—within 90 days after disablement or death and claimant knows/should know relation to employment.	Same as for accidents	Unlimited	Same as for accidents. Pneumoconiosis—partial disability less than 33-1/3% is noncompensable**
KANSAS	All diseases		Disability or death—within 1 year after last exposure (3 years for death from silicosis, 7 years for death following continuous disability). Does not apply to radiation. Silicosis presumed nonoccupational absent exposure in 5 years over 10 years prior to disability (2 of 5 years in-state unless same employer); employer liable only if exposure lasts 60 days.	Within 1 year after disablement, death, or last payment (2 years after last payment in case of silicosis). Radiation—within 1 year after claimant knows/should know relation to employment.		Unlimited	Same as for accidents*

KENTUCKY	All diseases*			Disability—within 3 years after last exposure or first manifestation. Death—within 3 years, if it occurs within 3 years after last exposure or first manifestation. Limit waived where voluntary payment or employer knows of disease and cause. No claim more than 5 years after last exposure (20 years in case of radiation or asbestos-related disease),** except for death within 20 years after continuous disability begins in cases where there is award or timely claim for disability.		Unlimited	Same as for accidents. Where disablement occurs after 5 years' exposure or results from silicosis or pneumoconiosis, apportioned between employer and Special Fund: Fund pays 75% of cost if not conclusively proven to result from last exposure, otherwise pays 40%. Employer pays balance.
LOUISIANA	All diseases		Diseases contracted in less than 1 year presumed to be nonoccupational. Presumption is rebuttable by "overwhelming preponderance of evidence."	Disability—within 6 months after manifestation, occurrence of disability, or worker knows/should know relation to employment. Death—within 6 months, or within 6 months after worker knows/should know relation to employment.	Same as for accidents	Unlimited	Same as for accidents
MAINE	All diseases		Incapacity—within 3 years after last exposure (does not apply to asbestos-related disease). Employer liable only if exposure lasts 60 days (except for radiation and asbestos-related disease). Silicosis presumed nonoccupational absent in-state exposure in 2 years during 15 years preceding disability (part of exposure may be out of state if same employer).*	Within 2 years after incapacity or 1 year after death or last payment (40 years after last payment for asbestos-related disease).** If mistake of fact, within reasonable time but no later than 10 years after last payment. Radiation—limit runs from date of incapacity and claimant knows/should know relation to employment.	Disability payments	Unlimited	Same as for accidents
MARYLAND	All diseases*			Any action for damages from occupational disease—within 3 years of discovery that occupational disease was cause of illness or death, but not later than 10 years.		Unlimited	Same as for accidents
MASSACHUSETTS	All diseases			Within 1 year after injury, or death; excusable.	Disability payments	Unlimited	Same as for accidents

Idaho *Silicosis—worker who is affected but not disabled may waive full compensation and, if later disabled, receive benefits up to $5,000.

Ind. *20 years if last asbestos dust exposure occurs on or after 7/1/85, 3 years if last exposure occurred before 7/1/85.

Iowa *Death from respiratory disease of coalminer employed 10 years presumed due to pneumoconiosis.
**Effective 7/1/84, 33% threshold requirement repealed; benefits now payable are prospective only.

Kan. *Worker who is affected but not disabled may waive full compensation and if later disabled receive benefits up to 100 weeks.

Iowa *Death from respiratory disease of coalminer employed 10 years presumed due to pneumoconiosis.
**Effective 7/1/84, 33% threshold requirement repealed; benefits now payable are prospective only.

Kan. *Worker who is affected but not disabled may waive full compensation and if later disabled receive benefits up to 100 weeks.

Ky. *Black lung claimant must file under state and federal law.
**Applies to asbestos-related disease claims filed on or after 7/15/86.

Me. *Asbestos-related diseases not covered by Maine Act if at time of last injurious exposure the employee was covered by Federal Longshore Act or FELA.
**Claim for asbestos-related disease contracted between 11/30/67 and 10/1/83 must be filed by 1/1/85.

Md. *Disease or injury compensable under federal law (other than Social Security Disability Insurance) is not compensable.

CHART IV □ COVERAGE OF OCCUPATIONAL DISEASES □ January 1, 1989 (continued)

JURISDICTION	NATURE OF COVERAGE[1]	MEDICAL BOARDS	ONSET OF DISABILITY OR DEATH	TIME LIMIT ON CLAIM FILING	DEDUCTIONS FROM DEATH AWARDS	MEDICAL CARE	COMPENSATION[2]
MICHIGAN	All diseases			Within 2 years after claimant knows/should know relation to employment.		Unlimited	Same as for accidents*
MINNESOTA	All diseases*			Within 3 years after employee's knowledge of cause of injury and disability.		Unlimited	Same as for accidents. Non-disabled claimants eligible for medical benefits. Supplemental benefits may be payable after 4 years from date of injury.
MISSISSIPPI	All diseases			Within 2 years after injury* or death.	Same as for accidents	Unlimited	Same as for accidents
MISSOURI	All diseases		Last employer liable regardless of length of time of last exposure.	Within 2 years after injury, death, or last payment (3 years if no injury report filed); limitation runs from date injury is reasonably apparent.	Disability payments	Unlimited	Same as for accidents
MONTANA	All diseases	Examinations made by 1 or more members of the occupational disease panel.	Death—within 3 years after last employment unless continuous total disability (does not apply to radiation).	Within 2 years after disability and claimant knows/should know relation to employment; may be extended 2 more years.*	Disability payments	Unlimited	Same as for accidents, excluding partial disability. Worker who is affected but not disabled may leave job and receive compensation up to $10,000. Pneumoconiosis benefits reduced by amount payable under federal law. Silicosis victims or beneficiaries not qualifying for occupational disease benefits may receive up to $200 monthly; supplement is resource indemnity trust financed.
NEBRASKA	All diseases			Within 2 years after knew/should have known of injury and relation to employment.		Unlimited	Same as for accidents
NEVADA	All diseases	Medical review board selected by director; findings conclusive.	Silicosis or respiratory dust disease is noncompensable absent in-state exposure in 3 years during 10 years preceding disability or death.	Within 90 days after knowledge of disability and relation to employment or 1 year after death. Silicosis or respiratory dust disease—within 1 year after temporary or total disability or death.		Unlimited	Same as for accidents
NEW HAMPSHIRE	All diseases			Within 2 years after injury or death and claimant knows/should know of injury and relation to employment.*	Disability payments	Unlimited	Same as for accidents

NEW JERSEY	All diseases			Within 2 years after claimant knows relation to employment or last payment.		Unlimited	Same as for accidents
NEW MEXICO	All diseases		Death—within 1 year after last employment (3 years for death following continuous disability), and death must follow disability within 2 years. Silicosis or asbestosis—disability or death within 2 years after last employment (5 years for death following continuous disability); employer is liable only if exposure lasts 60 days; noncompensable absent in-state exposure in 1250 workshifts during 10 years preceding disability. Radiation—disability or death within 10 years after last employment.	Within 1 year after disability or death or 1 year 31 days after last voluntary payment. Radiation—within 1 year after disability begins or death and claimant knows/should know relation to employment.	Disability payments	Unlimited	Same as for accidents
NEW YORK	All diseases			Within 2 years after disablement or death, or two years after claimant knows/should know relation to employment.		Unlimited	Same as for accidents*
NORTH CAROLINA	All diseases	Commission appoints 3-member advisory board for silicosis or asbestosis cases.	Death within 2 years after injury; if totally disabled 6 years after injury or 2 years after final determination. Asbestosis—disability or death within 10 years after last exposure; for death following continuous disability, disability must occur within 10 years after last exposure.* Lead poisoning—disability or death within 2 years after last exposure; for death following continuous disability, disability must occur within 2 years after last exposure.	Within 2 years after final determination of disability or within 6 years after death from occupational disease.		Unlimited	Same as for accidents**
NORTH DAKOTA	All diseases		Death—within 1 year after injury if no disability, or 1 year after cessation of disability, or 6 years after injury if disability is continuous.*	Within 1 year after injury; within 2 years after death (2 years after injury if no claim prior to death).*		Unlimited	Same as for accidents

Mich. *Silicosis, dust disease, and logging industry fund reimburses compensation over $25,000 or 104 weeks, whichever is greater for injury after 6/30/85; also reimburses benefits in cases of exposure to brominated biphenyl before 7/24/79 and where disability or death occurs/becomes known after 7/24/79.

Minn. *Employer and insurer during last significant exposure liable.

Miss. *For radiation, date of disablement is date of injury.

Mont. *Claimant who is discharged or transferred to avoid liability may receive compensation when totally disabled up to $10,000.

N.H. *Date of injury is last date of exposure or first date worker knows/should know relation to employment.

N.Y. *Disability or death due to silicosis or dust disease reimbursed from special fund for all payments over 104 weeks.

N.C. *Asbestosis or silicosis is noncompensable absent in-state exposure in 2 years during 10 years preceding last exposure or if exposure is less than 30 working days in 7 consecutive months.

**Worker who is affected but not disabled by asbestosis or silicosis or who is removed from exposure receives benefits up to $80 weekly for 104 weeks. If later totally disabled, full compensation is paid. If death results within 2 years after last exposure (350 weeks if caused by secondary infection), full compensation is paid. If partially disabled, 66-2/3% of wage loss is paid for another 196 weeks. If unrelated death, balance of 104 weeks is paid plus 300 weeks (total disability) or percentage of 196 weeks (partial disability). Worker may waive full compensation and receive 104 weeks of compensation plus 100 more weeks if later disabled or dies.

N.D. *Date of injury is date on which a reasonable person knows/should know relation to employment.

CHART IV ☐ COVERAGE OF OCCUPATIONAL DISEASES ☐ January 1, 1989 (continued)

JURISDICTION	NATURE OF COVERAGE[1]	MEDICAL BOARDS	ONSET OF DISABILITY OR DEATH	TIME LIMIT ON CLAIM FILING	DEDUCTIONS FROM DEATH AWARDS	MEDICAL CARE	COMPENSATION[2]
OHIO	All diseases	Medical specialist in specific cases; findings advisory.		Within 2 years after disability or death or within 6 months after diagnosis (whichever is later).		Unlimited	Same as for accidents. No partial disability for respiratory dust disease.*
OKLAHOMA	All diseases		Employer liable for silicosis or asbestosis only if exposure lasts 60 days.	Within 2 years after last exposure or manifestation and diagnosis by a physician.		Unlimited	Same as for accidents*
OREGON	All diseases			Within one year of worker's discovery of disease, after disablement, or physician informs claimant of the disease.		Unlimited	Same as for accidents
PENNSYLVANIA	All diseases	Examination by impartial physician may be ordered.	Within 300 weeks after last exposure (except death following disability that occurs within 300 weeks after last exposure). Silicosis, anthracosilicosis, or coalminer's pneumoconiosis—noncompensable absent in-state exposure in 2 years during 10 years preceding disability.*	Within 3 years after disablement, death, or last payment. Radiation—within 3 years after the employee knows/should know relation to employment.		Unlimited	Same as for accidents*
PUERTO RICO	All diseases		Disability—within 1 year after last exposure, except diseases with longer latency periods.	Within 3 years from time employee learns nature of disability and relation to work or could have learned through reasonable diligence.		Unlimited	Same as for accidents
RHODE ISLAND	All diseases	Director of Workers' Compensation appoints one or more impartial physicians; any commissioner can appoint impartial examiner.	Disability date determined by the Department or by the Commissioner.	Within 3 years from date of discovery. Radiation—within 1 year after claimant knows/should know relation to employment.		Unlimited	Same as for accidents
SOUTH CAROLINA	All diseases	Medical board determines controverted medical questions; pulmonary cases may be referred to pulmonary specialist of state medical universities.	Disease must be contracted within 1 year after last exposure (2 years for pulmonary dust disease), except radiation. Byssinosis is noncompensable absent exposure for 7 years.	Within 2 years after definitive diagnosis or 2 years after death. Radiation—limitation runs from date of disability and claimant knows/should know relation to employment.	Disability payments	Unlimited	Same as for accidents. Worker who is affected but not disabled may waive compensation (except radiation).
SOUTH DAKOTA	All diseases	Division may contract with physicians for reports.	Silicosis—noncompensable absent in-state exposure in 2 years (in-state requirement waived if same employer); employer liable only if exposure lasts 60 days.	Within 2 years after disability or death. Radiation—within 1 year after disability and claimant knows relation to employment.	Disability payments	Unlimited	Same as for accidents. No permanent partial disability for silicosis.*

TENNESSEE	All diseases			Within 1 year after incapacity or death.	Same as for accidents	Unlimited	Same as for accidents. Coalminer's pneumoconiosis—same as federal Black Lung Act.
TEXAS	All diseases	Provides for medical committee to pass on controverted questions and with power to order examinations.		Within 1 year after injury or first distinct manifestation, 1 year after death. May be extended.	Same as for accidents		Same as for accidents
UTAH	All diseases	Commission appoints medical panel of 1 or more to report on extent of disability.	Partial disability—within 2 years after last exposure. Total disability—within 1 year after last employment; for silicosis, 3 years (uncomplicated) or 5 years (complicated). Death—within 3 years after last employment (5 years for complicated silicosis or death following continuous total disability). Not applicable to radiation. Silicosis—noncompensable absent 5 years in-state exposure in 15 years preceding disability; employer liable only if exposure lasts 30 days.	Within 1 year after incapacity or death and claimant knows/should know relation to employment, but no later than 3 years after death. Permanent partial disability—within 2 years.	Disability payments	Unlimited	Same as for accidents*
VERMONT	All diseases		Disablement—within 5 years after last exposure. Death—during employment or after continuous disability beginning within 5 years after last exposure, but no later than 12 years after last exposure. Does not apply to radiation.	Within 1 year after discovery, death, or last payment. Radiation—within 1 year after first incapacity and worker knew/should have known relation to employment.		Unlimited	Same as for accidents. Affected but nondisabled worker may waive full compensation and later receive limited compensation.
VIRGIN ISLANDS	All diseases			Within 60 days after disability.		Same as for accidents.	Same as for accidents
VIRGINIA	All occupational diseases and some ordinary diseases of life under unusual evidentiary standards of proof.		Exposure in 90 workshifts conclusive as to injurious exposure only for pneumoconiosis.	Within 2 years after diagnosis is first communicated to worker, or within 5 years after last exposure, whichever is first.* Within 3 years after death occurring within periods for disability.	Disability payments	Unlimited	Same as for accidents.** Worker who is affected but not disabled may waive compensation.
WASHINGTON	All diseases			Within 2 years after employee left service with the employer.		Unlimited	Same as for accidents

Ohio *Includes asbestosis, silicosis, and coalminer's pneumoconiosis. Worker who is affected but not disabled by respiratory dust disease and leaves employment may receive $49 weekly for 30 weeks, then 66-2/3% of wage loss (not to exceed $40.25 weekly).

Okla. *Worker who is affected but not disabled by silicosis or asbestosis may waive compensation for aggravation of disease and, if later disabled, receive benefits for 100 weeks up to $2,000.

Pa. *Under Occupational Disease Act, state pays $125 monthly for total disability or death caused by silicosis, anthracosilicosis, coalminer's pneumoconiosis, or asbestosis, provided there has been 2 years of in-state exposure, in cases where the claim is barred by the statute of limitations and the last exposure occurred before 1965 or where exposure occurred under several employers.

S.D. *Worker who is affected by silicosis but not disabled may waive full compensation and if later disabled or dies receive benefits up to 52 times the maximum weekly benefit; if leaves employment, may receive compensation up to $1,000.

Utah *Worker with permanent partial disability who must change occupation may receive up to $1,000 for vocational rehabilitation and retraining, plus compensation of 66-2/3% of average weekly wages up to 66-2/3% of SAWW for up to 20 weeks, then additional compensation (cumulative total may not exceed $2,080).

Va. *5-year limitation does not apply to cataract of the eyes, skin cancer, radium disability, ulceration, undulant fever, angiosarcoma of the liver due to vinyl chloride exposure, or mesothelioma; byssinosis—within 7 years after last exposure; coalminer's pneumoconiosis—within 3 years after diagnosis; asbestosis—within 2 years after diagnosis or if based on changed condition, within 2 years after diagnosis of advanced stage. No claim for an advanced stage of asbestosis shall be denied on the ground that there has been no subsequent accident.
**Compensation for advanced asbestosis based on wages at a time of diagnosis if employed in same employment where injurious exposure occured; otherwise based on average weekly wage of worker in similar employment.

CHART IV ☐ COVERAGE OF OCCUPATIONAL DISEASES ☐ January 1, 1989 (continued)

JURISDICTION	NATURE OF COVERAGE[1]	MEDICAL BOARDS	ONSET OF DISABILITY OR DEATH	TIME LIMIT ON CLAIM FILING	DEDUCTIONS FROM DEATH AWARDS	MEDICAL CARE	COMPENSATION[2]
WEST VIRGINIA	All diseases	Occupational Pneumoconiosis Board appointed by Commissioner determines medical questions.	Occupational pneumoconiosis is non-compensable absent 2 years continuous exposure in 10 years before last exposure or 5 years cumulative exposure within 15 years before date of last exposure.	Within 3 years after knowledge or last exposure. Within 2 years after death.		Unlimited	Same as for accidents
WISCONSIN	All diseases	May appoint independent medical expert in doubtful cases.	Disability date is last day of work for last employer whose employment caused disability.	Unlimited. After 12 years claim may be filed with state fund.		Unlimited	Same as for accidents
WYOMING	All diseases	Yes		Within 1 year after diagnosis or 3 years after exposure, whichever is last. Radiation—within 1 year after diagnosis or death.	Disability payments	Unlimited	Same as for accidents
F.E.C.A.	All diseases			Within 3 years after injury, death, or disability and claimant knows/should know relation to employment; excusable		Unlimited	Same as for accidents
LONGSHORE ACT	All diseases			Within 1 year after injury, death, last payment, or knowledge of relation to employment		Unlimited	Same as for accidents*

Longshore *In permanent partial disabilty claims due to occupational disease where times of injury occurs after retirement, compensation is 66⅔ of average weekly wage times percentage of permanent impairment (according to AMA guidelines) payable while impairment continues.

APPENDIX C
Income Benefits for Total Disability*

* Source: U.S. Chamber of Commerce, 1989 Analysis of Workers' Compensation Laws, "Chart VI, Income Benefits for Total Disability, January 1, 1989," pp. 18–20.

CHART VI INCOME BENEFITS FOR TOTAL DISABILITY January 1, 1989

JURISDICTION	PERCENT OF WAGES	MAXIMUM WEEKLY PAYMENT		MINIMUM WEEKLY PAYMENT		TIME LIMIT	AMOUNT LIMIT[2]	AUTOMATIC COST OF LIVING INCREASE	OFFSETS[3]	NOTATIONS
		AMOUNT	RATE	AMOUNT	RATE					
ALABAMA	66-2/3	$ 344.00	100% SAWW	$94.60[1]	27.5% SAWW[1]	Disability				Annual increase in maximum effective July 1.*
ALASKA	80% of spendable earnings	700.00		110.00*		Disability			Social Security, unemployment compensation, employer-funded pension or profit sharing plan	Annual increase in maximum effective January 1.
AMERICAN SAMOA	66-2/3	205.00		40.00		Disability				Compensation increased 10% if installment without award unpaid after 14 days, 20% if installment following award unpaid after 10 days.
ARIZONA	66-2/3	253.19				TT—Disability PT—Life				Benefits payable monthly. Additional $10 monthly if 1 or more total dependents, not subject to maximum.
ARKANSAS	66-2/3	209.00*	66-2/3% SAWW	20.00		TT—450 weeks PT—Disability	TT—94,086**		Unemployment compensation, Social Security	25% penalty for employer's violation of safety laws.***
CALIFORNIA	66-2/3	224.00		112.00		TT—Disability PT—Life		TT—after 2 years	Umemployment compensation, Social Security	50% increased compensation if injury due to employer's serious, willful misconduct.
COLORADO	66-2/3	354.69	80% SAWW			TT—Disability* PT—Life			Social Security, unemployment compensation	Annual increase in maximum effective July 1. Compensation increased 50% if employer failed to comply with insurance provisions. Compensation decreased 50% if injury results from worker's failure to obey safety regulations or from intoxication.
CONNECTICUT	66-2/3	671.00	150% SAWW	134.20*	20% maximum	Disability		October 1		Annual increase in maximum effective October 1. Additional $10 weekly per dependent child under 18, maximum 50% of basic benefit or 75% of wage (whichever is less). Compensation increased to 75% of wages if employer violated OSHA regulation.**
DELAWARE	66-2/3	265.14	66-2/3% SAWW	88.38[1]	22-2/9% SAWW[1]	Disability				Annual increase in maximum effective July 1.
DISTRICT OF COLUMBIA	66-2/3 up to 80% of spendable earnings*	513.00*	100% SAWW*	128.25*	25% SAWW*	Disability		PT—October 1, maximum 5%*	Social Security, employer-funded pension	Annual increase in maximum effective January 1*.
FLORIDA	66-2/3	362.00	100% SAWW	20.00		TT-350 weeks PT-Disability	TT—*126,700*		Unemployment compensation, Social Security	Annual increase in maximum effective January 1. Compensation increased 10% if installment unpaid after 14 days.*

GEORGIA	66-2/3	175.00*		25.00[1]		Disability				Board may assess penalties of not more than $1,000, or less than $100 for refusal, unreasonable delay, or willful neglect to make payment.*
GUAM	66-2/3	140.00	66-2/3% SAWW	50.00[1]		Disability	40,000			Compensation increased 10% for late payment without award; 20% if award.
HAWAII	66-2/3	358.00	100% SAWW	TT—90.00* PT—90.00	TT—25% SAWW* PT—25% SAWW	Disability		PT—injuries prior to June 18, 1980		Annual increase in maximum effective January 1. Compensation may be increased 10% for failure to pay within 31 days after decision or award, or within 10 business days for uncontroverted temporary total disability case.
IDAHO	60	290.70 to 403.75	90% SAWW	145.35	45% SAWW	Disability		After 52 weeks		Annual increase in maximum effective January 1. For first 52 weeks benefit is 60% of worker's wages if there are no dependent children under 18; after 52 weeks benefit is 60% of SAWW. Benefit is increased 7% of SAWW per dependent child (up to 5), but may not exceed 90% of wages. 8% interest on late payments.
ILLINOIS	66-2/3	580.89	133-1/3% SAWW	TT—100.90* PT—217.84	PT—50% SAWW	TT—Disability PT—Life		PT—July 15 of 2nd year		Semiannual increases in maximum effective January 15 and July 15.**
INDIANA	66-2/3	256.00*		50.00[1]		500 weeks	128,000*			After 500 weeks, additional benefits are payable from second injury fund in 150-week increments.***
IOWA	80% of spendable earnings	660.00	200% SAWW	115.50*	35% SAWW*	Disability				Annual increase in maximum effective July 1. Benefits increased 50% if late or stopped without good cause.
KANSAS	66-2/3	263.00	75% SAWW	25.00		Disability	TT—100,000 PT—125,000 (includes TT)			Annual increase in maximum effective July 1. Compensation may be increased up to $100 per week past due (plus up to $25 per week past due for failure to pay medical bill).
KENTUCKY	66-2/3*	345.02	100% SAWW	69.00	20% SAWW	Disability				Annual increase in maximum effective January 1. Compensation increased or decreased 15% if injury caused by safety violation. 12% interest on late payments.

[1]Actual weekly wage if less.

[2]Amounts shown in italics have been calculated.

[3]Social Security offsets generally apply by formula up to 50% of basic benefit.

Ala. *Compensation may be increased up to 10% for failure to pay within 30 days after due.

Alaska *Spendable weekly earnings if less.

Ariz. *Maximum monthly wages are $1650 for employees injured from 12/31/87 to 6/30/89. Increased to $1800 per month on 7/1/89 and $2100 on 7/1/91.

Ark. *Maximum effective until 12/31/89. As of 1/1/90, maximum weekly benefits will be increased to 70% SAWW.
**18% penalty for failure to pay without an award, 20% penalty for failure to pay with an award.

Colo. *TT payments cease when claimant reaches maximum medical improvement, is able to return to work, or as otherwise determined by Director.

Conn *80% of average weekly wages, if less.
**12% interest benefits added if undue delay in payment; 6% if undue delay in adjustment (4 weeks presumed undue delay).

D.C. *Maximum is no less than $513.00; minimum is 25% SAWW or 80% of actual earnings if less. Benefits for D.C. government employees are similar to F.E.C.A.

Fla. *Compensation increased 20% if unpaid 30 days after award.

Ga. *Income payable without award increased 15% if not paid within 14 days unless claim is controverted or Board excuses. Awarded benefits increased 20% if not paid within 20 days unless Board grants review.

Hawaii *Actual wages if less, but no less than $38.

Ill. *Minimum TT benefit is $100.90 if unmarried and ranges up to $124.30 if 4 or more dependents. In all cases claimant receives actual weekly wage if less.
**TT benefits may be increased $10 per day, up to $2,500, for unreasonable delay in payment; 14 days is presumed unreasonable. Compensation may be increased 50% for unreasonable or vexatious delay in payment. Compensation may be increased 25% for employer's willful violation of safety standard.

Ind. *Effective 7/1/88. Increased to $411 on 7/1/89 and to $441 on 7/1/90. TTD benefits are subject to child support withholdings.
**Increased to $137,000 on 7/1/89 and $147,000 on 7/1/90.
***Award is increased 5% if employer loses on court appeal; court may increase to 10%.

Iowa *Employee's spendable earnings if less.

Ky. *80% of AWW during rehabilitation.

CHART VI ☐ INCOME BENEFITS FOR TOTAL DISABILITY ☐ January 1, 1989 (continued)

JURISDICTION	PERCENT OF WAGES	MAXIMUM WEEKLY PAYMENT		MINIMUM WEEKLY PAYMENT		TIME LIMIT	AMOUNT LIMIT[2]	AUTOMATIC COST OF LIVING INCREASE	OFFSETS[3]	NOTATIONS
		AMOUNT	RATE	AMOUNT	RATE					
LOUISIANA	66-2/3	$ 267.00	75% SAWW	71.00	20% SAWW[1]	Disability			Social Security,* unemployment compensation, employer-funded disability, federal workers' compensation	Annual increase in maximum effective September 1. Penalty of $200 or 15% on late payments.
MAINE	66-2/3	447.92*	(*)	$25.00**			(**)	For injuries on or after 11/20/87, on anniversary of date of injury beginning with 3rd anniversary.	Employer funded benefits, old age Social Security, unemployment benefits.	Annual increase in maximum effective July 1.
MARYLAND	66-2/3	407.00	100% SAWW	TT—50.00[1]		Disability	45,000	PT-January 1, maximum 5%		Annual increase in maximum effective July 1. If permanent disability exceeds 50% of whole body, worker receives additional compensation from Subsequent Injury Fund after completion of payments by employer.
MASSACHUSETTS	66-2/3	444.20	100% SAWW	TT-20.00* PT-88.84	PT-20% SAWW	Disability	TT—115,492**		Unemployment compensation, pension, old age Social Security	Annual increase in maximum effective October 1. Additional $6 weekly per dependent if total benefit does not exceed $150 or 100% of wages.***
MICHIGAN	80% of spendable earnings	409.00	90% SAWW	PT-113.61	PT—25% SAWW	Disability*			Disability, unemployment compensation, pension, old age Social Security retirement**	Annual increase in maximum effective January 1. Additional $50 per day for award unpaid after 30 days, maximum $1,500.
MINNESOTA	66-2/3	391.00	100% SAWW	195.50	50% SAWW*	TT-90 days after maximum medical improvement or end of retraining		Anniversary of injury	Social Security after $25,000 paid for PTD.**	Annual increase in maximum effective October 1. Late payment may be increased 10% if inexcusably delayed, plus interest.
MISSISSIPPI	66-2/3	198.00*	66-2/3% SAWW	25.00		450 weeks	*89,100**			Annual increase in maximum effective January 1. Additional rehabilitation allowance up to $10 weekly for 52 weeks.
MISSOURI	66-2/3	279.64	75% SAWW	40.00		TT—400 weeks PT—Life	TT—*111,856*			Annual increase in maximum effective July 1. 8% interest for late payments.*
MONTANA	66-2/3	299.00	100% SAWW			Disability*		As of 7/1/90, max of 10 annual COLA adjustments rate no more than % increase in SAWW or 3%, whichever is less	Social Security	Annual increase in maximum effective July 1. PT benefits may be paid out in a lump sum, subject to a discount to present value based on average rate for U.S. 10-year treasury bills. Advances limited to $20,000. Compensation may be increased 20% if payment unreasonably delayed or refused.

NEBRASKA	66-2/3	245.00		49.00[1]		Disability				
NEVADA	66-2/3	368.82	100% SAWW			TT—Disability PT—Life			Social Security	TT benefits payable bi-weekly. PT benefits payable monthly.* Annual increase in maximum effective July 1.
NEW HAMPSHIRE	66-2/3	559.50	150% SAWW	149.20[1]	40% SAWW[1]	Disability		July 1—after 3 years		Annual increase in maximum effective July 1. Double compensation if employer violated prior recorded safety standard.
NEW JERSEY	70	342.00	75% SAWW	91.00	20% SAWW	TT—400 weeks PT—Life	TT—*136,800*		Social Security	Annual increase in maximum effective January 1. After 450 weeks at reduced rate if employed; at full rate if not able to be rehabilitated.
NEW MEXICO	66-2/3	283.70	85% SAWW	36.00[1]		700 weeks*	*198,590*		Unemployment benefits	Annual increase in maximum effective January 1. 10% additional compensation payable by employer for failure to provide safety devices. 10% decrease for failure to use provided safety device.
NEW YORK	66-2/3	300.00		TT—20.00[1] PT—30.00[1]		Disability			Social Security	Persons receiving PT benefits may collect full compensation and wages, but not in excess of pre-injury wage base.
NORTH CAROLINA	66-2/3	376.00	110% SAWW	30.00		TT—Disability PT—Life			Unemployment benefits	Increases in maximum effective January 1 and July 1.
NORTH DAKOTA	66-2/3	306.00 plus dependents	100% SAWW	183.60[1]	60% SAWW[1]	Disability			Social Security	Annual increase in maximum effective July 1. Additional $10 weekly per dependent child under 18, or to age 22 if child is attending a full-time educational institution; total benefits may not exceed claimant's net take-home pay.
OHIO	72—first 12 weeks 66-2/3—after 12 weeks	400.00*	100% SAWW	TT—133.33[1] PT—200.00[1]	TT—33-1/3% SAWW[1] PT—50% SAWW[1]	TT—Disability** PT—Life			Employer funded benefits	Annual increase in maximum effective January 1. If PT benefit plus Social Security are less than $161.92 weekly, Disabled Workers' Relief Fund pays the lesser of the difference between the DWRF rate and PT or the DWRF rate and social security; amount increased annually by increase in Consumer Price Index.

La. *PT benefits reduced so that combined Social Security and PT benefits do not exceed 80% of pre-injury wages.

Maine *Frozen at $447.92 until 6/30/89.
**Employee who has reached maximum medical improvement and is able to perform full-time remunerative work in the ordinary competitive labor market in the state not eligible for total disability benefits, but may receive partial.
***Carrier may be assessed up to $100 per day for failure to pay award within 10 days.

Mass. *Actual wages if less, but no less than $20 if working at least 15 hours a week.
**260 times SAWW; includes permanent partial disability.
***Double compensation if injury due to employer's serious and willful misconduct. If no benefits are paid prior to to final decision of claim, award is based on benefits in effect at time of decision instead of date of injury.
Eligible for supplementary benefits after 24 months, calculated on October 1, equal to base benefit times percent increase in SAWW over SAWW at time of injury.

Mich. *Conclusive presumption of PT disability does not extend beyond 800 weeks from injury; thereafter determined in accordance with facts.
**Benefits reduced if claimant is eligible for Social Security and such benefits are not being coordinated.

Minn. *Actual wages if less, but not less than 20% of SAWW; $78.20 through 9/30/89. After 208 weeks' total disability, supplementary benefits bring compensation to 65% of SAWW; $254.15 through 9/30/89.
**Other government disability benefits from same injury also offset.

Miss. *Effective 7/1/88.

Mo. *Compensation increased 15% if injury caused by failure to comply with statute or order, decreased 15% if caused by worker's failure to use safety device.

Mont. *Compensation terminates upon receipt of or eligibility for Social Security retirement benefits.

Nevada *Maximum monthly wages on which benefits are computed are $2,395.49, effective 7/1/88.

N.M. *Except for total disability resulting from primary mental impairment in which case the maximum period is 100 weeks.

Ohio *Maximum PT rate is 66⅔% SAWW unless claimant receives Social Security, which, combined with PT, brings maximum up to 100% SAWW.
**After 200 weeks claimant examined to determine if disability is permanent.

CHART VI □ INCOME BENEFITS FOR TOTAL DISABILITY □ January 1, 1989 (continued)

JURISDICTION	PERCENT OF WAGES	MAXIMUM WEEKLY PAYMENT		MINIMUM WEEKLY PAYMENT		TIME LIMIT	AMOUNT LIMIT[2]	AUTOMATIC COST OF LIVING INCREASE	OFFSETS[3]	NOTATIONS
		AMOUNT	RATE	AMOUNT	RATE					
OKLAHOMA	66-2/3	231.00	66-2/3% SAWW	30.00[1]		TT—150 weeks*	TT—*34,650*			Maximum amounts adjusted every three years, based on state average weekly wage.
OREGON	66-2/3	TT-370.96 PT-395.96	100% SAWW	50.00*		Disability			PT—Social Security	Annual increase in maximum effective July 1. Additional $5 weekly per dependent for PT (up to 5).
PENNSYLVANIA	66-2/3	399.00	100% SAWW	199.50*	50% SAWW*	Disability				Annual increase in maximum effective January 1.
PUERTO RICO	66-2/3	46.15		15.00		TT—312 weeks PT—Life	*24,300*			Compensation doubled if due to employer's violation of safety or health law or regulation.
RHODE ISLAND	66-2/3	360.00 plus 9.00 per dependent	100% SAWW			Disability				Annual increase in maximum effective September 1. Additional $9 per dependent child under 18; total benefit may not exceed 80% of pre-injury wages.*
SOUTH CAROLINA	66-2/3	334.87	100% SAWW	75.00[1]		500 weeks*	*167,435**			Annual increase in maximum effective January 1.
SOUTH DAKOTA	66-2/3	281.00	100% SAWW	141.00[1]	50% SAWW[1]	TT—Disability PT—Life		July 1st, for injuries on or after 7/1/88		Annual increase in maximum effective July 1.
TENNESSEE	66-2/3	231.00*		35.00		TT—Disability PT—400 weeks	92,400			After 400 weeks PT benefit is reduced to $15. Compensation may be increased 25% for failure to pay claim.
TEXAS	66-2/3	238.00	(**)	$39.00	(**)	401 weeks*	*95,438*			Annual increase in maximum effective September 1.**
UTAH	66-2/3	TT—344.00 PT—292.00	TT—100% SAWW PT— 85% SAWW	45.00[1]		Disability*			Social Security	Annual increase in maximum effective July 1. Additional $5 if spouse, plus $5 per dependent child under 18 (up to 4); total benefit may not exceed maximum.*
VERMONT	66-2/3	514.00 plus dependents	150% SAWW	171.00[1]	50% SAWW[1]	Disability*		July 1		Annual increase in maximum effective July 1. Additional $10 per dependent child under 21; total benefits may not exceed pre-injury wages.**
VIRGIN ISLANDS	TT—66-2/3* PT—75	193.00*	66-2/3% SAWW*	60.00[1,*]		Disability		After 2 years on January 1		Annual increase in maximum effective January 1. Total disability benefits begin after medical and vocational rehabilitation end. Compensation increased 15% for injury caused by employer's failure to obey safety order.*

VIRGINIA	66-2/3	362.00	100% SAWW	90.50[1]	25% SAWW[1]	TT—500 weeks PT—Disability*	TT—*181,000*	October 1**		Annual increase in maximum effective July 1. Compensation increased 20% for failure to pay within 2 weeks after due.
WASHINGTON	60 to 75, depending on conjugal status	384.26	100% SAWW	43.02*		Disability		July 1	Social Security under age 65. Disability, Retirement.	Benefits payable monthly. Annual increase in maximum effective July 1. 60% of wage, additional 5% of wages for spouse, plus 2% of wages per dependent child (up to 5), up to maximum.
WEST VIRGINIA	70	358.52	100% SAWW	119.51	33-1/3% SAWW	TT—208 weeks PT—Life	TT—*74,572*			All but TT benefits payable monthly. Annual adjustment in maximum effective July 1.
WISCONSIN	66-2/3	363.00	100% SAWW	30.00		TT—Disability PT—Life			Social Security	Annual increase in maximum effective January 1.*
WYOMING	TT—66-2/3	TT—356.19 PT—237.47 plus dependents	66-2/3% of actual not to exceed SAW for quarter	PT—237.47	PT—66-2/3% SAWW	TT—Disability PT—Life	(*)			Benefits payable monthly. Quarterly increases in maximum effective January 1, April 1, July 1, and October 1. PT benefit fixed at 66-2/3% of SAMW plus $100 per child monthly.
F.E.C.A.	66-2/3 or 75	1071.68	66-2/3% or 75% of highest rate for GS-15	165.63[1]	66-2/3% or 75% of lowest rate for GS-2[1]	TT—Disability PT—Life		October 1	(*)	Benefits payable monthly. Increase effective 1/6/85. Higher percentage payable if 1 or more dependent.
LONGSHORE ACT	66-2/3	636.24*	200% NAWW*	159.06[1,*]	50% NAWW[1,*]	Disability		PT—October 1	Jones Act, other workers' compensation benefits	Annual increase in maximum effective October 1.

Oklahoma *Court order may extend benefits for up to 300 weeks.

Ore. *90% of actual wages, if less.

Pa. *90% of wages if less, but no less than 33⅓% of SAWW ($133.00, effective 1/1/89).

P.R. *May be paid in monthly installments of $65 to $200 for life; total sum not to exceed $24,300.

R.I. *No compensation for PT disability if worker is earning pre-injury wages. Lump sum benefits available after benefits have been received for 6 months.

S.C. *Person who is para or quadraplegic or has suffered brain damage shall receive PT benefits for life. Commission may not order lump sum payment in such cases.

Tenn. *From date injury is determined to be permanent.

Texas *For life in case of amputation or paralysis of two limbs, loss of vision in both eyes, or permanent insanity.
**Maximum increased $7 and minimum increased $1 per $10 increase in SAWW.

Utah *Disability beyond 312 weeks is payable from Employers' Reinsurance Fund, minimum 36% SAWW.

Vt. *PT benefits payable at least 330 weeks, after temporary disability benefits cease. After 330 weeks, PT benefits continue while there is lost earning capacity.
**Benefits may be disallowed if injury results from worker's failure to use safety device.

V.I. *During vocational rehabilitation, income benefits are 75% of AWW, maximum SAWW, minimum $75 or actual wages if less.

Va. *500-week limit for certain PT cases.
**Recipient of Social Security ineligible for cost of living increases.

Wash. *Maximum monthly wages are $1,652.33 for employees injured from 7/1/88 to 6/30/89 ($19,828 annually).

Wisc. *Compensation may be adjusted up or down by 15% (up to $15,000) for failure to use safety device or obey code or order. 10% interest payable on late payments. Employer, insurer, or both may be assessed penalty up to double the amount of compensation (not to exceed $15,000) for bad faith failure to make payments.

Wyo. *Hearing examiner must approve the extension of PT payments beyond 60 months.

F.E.C.A. *Civil Service Retirement and Disability Fund (CSRA) overpayments.

Longshore *Effective 9/29/84, Nonappropriated Fund Instrumentalities Act employees subject to same maximum/minimum weekly rates as employees covered under Longshore Act.

APPENDIX D
Fatalities—Income Benefits for Spouse and Children*

* Source: U.S. Chamber of Commerce, 1989 Analysis of Workers' Compensation Laws, "Chart VIII, Fatalities—Income Benefits for Spouse and Children, January 1, 1989," pp. 24–25.

CHART VIII FATALITIES—INCOME BENEFITS FOR SPOUSE AND CHILDREN January 1, 1989

JURISDICTION	PERCENT OF WAGES			MAXIMUM WEEKLY PAYMENT		MINIMUM PER WEEK SPOUSE ONLY	TIME LIMIT	AMOUNT LIMIT[1]		MAXIMUM BURIAL ALLOWANCE
	SPOUSE PLUS CHILDREN	SPOUSE ONLY	ONE CHILD ONLY	SPOUSE PLUS CHILDREN	SPOUSE ONLY			SPOUSE PLUS CHILDREN	SPOUSE ONLY	
ALABAMA	66-2/3	50	50	$ 344.00*	$ 344.00*	$94.60*	500 weeks 2,3	*$172,000*	*$172,000*	$1,000
ALASKA				700.00*	700.00*	110.00*	(2,4,**)			2,500
AMERICAN SAMOA	66-2/3	35	35	70.00	36.75	5.25[8]	(2,4)			1,000
ARIZONA	66-2/3	35	25	253.19	132.90		(2,4)			1,000
ARKANSAS	66-2/3	35	50	209.08*	209.08*	20.00	(2,4)	(**)	(**)	3,000
CALIFORNIA	66-2/3	66-2/3	66-2/3	224.00	224.00	112.00	(2)	95,000	70,000	2,000
COLORADO	66-2/3	66-2/3	66-2/3	354.69*	354.69*	88.67*	(2,4,**)			2,000
CONNECTICUT	66-2/3	66-2/3	66-2/3	671.00*	671.00*	134.20*	(2,3)			4,000
DELAWARE	80	66-2/3	66-2/3	318.16*	265.14*	88.38*	(2,4)			700**
DISTRICT OF COLUMBIA	66-2/3	50	50	513.00*	513.00*	(*)	(2,4)			1,000
FLORIDA	66-2/3	50	33-1/3	362.00*	362.00*	20.00[8]	(2,3)	100,000	100,000	2,500
GEORGIA	66-2/3	66-2/3	66-2/3	175.00*	175.00*	25.00[8]	400 weeks 2,3	*70,000*	65,000	5,000
GUAM	66-2/3*	35	35	140.00	73.50	31.50**	(2,4)	40,000	40,000	1,200
HAWAII	66-2/3	50	40	358.00*	269.00*	90.00*	(2,4)	(**)	(**)	5,370***
IDAHO				193.80*	145.35*	145.35*	500 weeks 2	*96,900*	*72,575*	3,000[7]
ILLINOIS	66-2/3	66-2/3	66-2/3	580.89*	580.89*	217.84*	20 years 2,4,**	(**)	(**)	1,750
INDIANA	66-2/3	66-2/3	66-2/3	256.00*	175.00*	75.00[8]	500 weeks 2,4	95,000*	95,000*	4,000*
IOWA	80% of spendable earnings	80% of spendable earnings	80% of spendable earnings	660.00*	660.00*		(2,4)			1,000
KANSAS	66-2/3	66-2/3	66-2/3	263.00*	263.00*	25.00	(2,6)	200,000	200,000	3,200
KENTUCKY	75	50	50	258.76*	172.51*	69.00*	(2,4)			2,500[7]
LOUISIANA	65	32-1/2	32-1/2	267.00*	267.00*	71.00*	(2,4)			3,000
MAINE[9]	66-2/3	66-2/3	66-2/3	447.92*	447.92*	25.00**	(2,3)			1,000
MARYLAND	66-2/3	66-2/3	66-2/3	407.00*	407.00*	50.00[8]	(2,4)			2,500**
MASSACHUSETTS	66-2/3*	66-2/3*	66-2/3*	444.20*	444.20*	150.00*	(2,4,**)	(**)	(**)	2,000
MICHIGAN	80% of spendable earnings	80% of spendable earnings	80% of spendable earnings	409.00*	409.00*	227.22*	500 weeks 2,6,**	(**)	*204,500**	1,500
MINNESOTA***	66-2/3	50	60	391.00*	391.00*		(2,**)			2,500
MISSISSIPPI[9]	66-2/3	35	25	198.00*	198.00*	25.00	450 weeks 2	89,100*	89,100*	2,000
MISSOURI	66-2/3	66-2/3	66-2/3	279.64*	279.64*	40.00	(2,4,**)			2,000
MONTANA	66-2/3	66-2/3	66-2/3	299.00*	299.00*	149.50*	500 weeks 2			1,400
NEBRASKA	75	66-2/3	66-2/3	245.00	245.00	49.00[8]	(2,4)			2,000
NEVADA	66-2/3	66-2/3	66-2/3	368.82*	368.82*		(2,4)			2,500[7]
NEW HAMPSHIRE	66-2/3	66-2/3	66-2/3	559.50*	559.50*	149.20*	(2,**)			3,000
NEW JERSEY	70	50	50	342.00*	342.00*	91.00*	(2,3,**)			2,000

NEW MEXICO	66-2/3	66-2/3	66-2/3	283.70*	283.70*	36.00	700 weeks[2,4]	*198,590*	*198,590*	3,000
NEW YORK	66-2/3	66-2/3	66-2/3	300.00**	300.00**	30.00	([2,4,*])			3,000

[1]Amount limits have been computed where not stipulated by law and are shown in italics. Disability payments deducted in all laws, except those of Arizona, Arkansas, California, Delaware, District of Columbia, Florida, Michigan, Minnesota, Mississippi, Missouri, Nevada, New York, North Dakota, Oregon, Washington, West Virginia, Wisconsin, Wyoming, F.E.C.A., and Longshore Act.

[2]To child until age 18 (16 in Manitoba, Newfoundland, Northwest Territories, Ontario, Saskatchewan, and Yukon; 19 in Alaska, Oregon (if in high school), and Wyoming; 18 in Michigan and 21 if in school in New Brunswick). If invalid, for duration of invalidity (for 15 years in Wisconsin; for period decedent would have supported child in Newfoundland, Prince Edward Island, and Yukon). If student, to age 21 in Colorado, British Columbia, New Brunswick, Nova Scotia, Prince Edward Island, Saskatchewan, and C.M.S.C.A.; 22 in Connecticut, Florida, Georgia, Hawaii, Kentucky, Missouri, Montana, Nevada, North Dakota, South Dakota, Tennessee, and Virgin Islands; 23 in D.C., Kansas, Louisiana, Maine, Maryland, Mississippi, New Mexico, New York, Oklahoma, Oregon, Pennsylvania, Rhode Island, South Carolina, Virginia, Washington, F.E.C.A., and Longshore Act; 25 in America Samoa, Arkansas, Delaware, Illinois, Iowa, Minnesota, Nebraska, New Hampshire, Ohio, Puerto Rico, Texas, West Virginia, Alberta, and Newfoundland; no age limit in Alaska (4 years only), Massachusetts, Vermont, Manitoba, Northwest Territories, Ontario, and Quebec.

[3]To spouse for life; compensation ceases on remarriage, (Georgia—to spouse until age 65 or 400 weeks, whichever is greater; Maine—if dependency on new spouse is proven).

[4]To spouse for life; 2 years' lump sum upon remarriage (but only if no children in Colorado, Illinois, Indiana, and Iowa) or balance of compensation if less (Indiana, New Mexico, and South Carolina). In Illinois, lump sum is paid upon remarriage only if there were no children *at time of death*.

[5]To spouse for life; 1 year's lump sum upon remarriage.

[6]To spouse for life; cash lump sum on remarriage: Kansas—100 weeks or balance if less; Michigan—$500 or balance if less; Oregon— 24 times monthly benefit; Washington—$7,500 or 50% of remaining annuity value if less; Manitoba—$3,600; New Brunswick—1 year's spouse's income; Northwest Territories—$8,712; Nova Scotia—$2,800; Prince Edward Island—$4,200; Yukon—$7,019.

[7]Additional allowance for transportation of body; no maximum except: Virginia—$500; Alberta—$450; British Columbia—$583.80 and $526.04 for incidental death expenses; Nova Scotia—$300; Prince Edward Island—$300; Yukon—$283; C.M.S.C.A.—$125.

[8]Actual wage if less.

[9]Spouse receives cash lump sum in addition to other benefits: Maine—$1,000; Mississippi—$250; North Dakota—$300 plus $100 per child; Oklahoma—$10,000 plus $2,500 per dependent (maximum $15,000); Washington—$800; Alberta—$1,100; British Columbia—$1,261.91; Manitoba—$1,305; Northwest Territories—$1,056; Nova Scotia—$1,000; Ontario—$1,500; Prince Edward Island—$500; Quebec—$1,177; Saskatchewan—$1,000; Yukon—$1,348; C.M.S.C.A.—$750.

[10]If no dependents.

[11]To spouse for 5 years or until youngest child reaches the age of 16. Benefits not interrupted upon remarriage.

[12]To spouse for life, regardless of remarriage.

Ala. *Maximum is 100% of SAWW; minimum is 27-1/2% of SAWW, actual wage if less.

Alaska *Maximum is set by statute.
**Spousal benefit reduced by 1/3 as of 5 years after worker's death, by 1/2 as of 8 years, and ceases after 10 years; reductions do not apply if spouse is over 52 or permanently and totally disabled. Limited Social Security offset.

Ariz. *Maximum monthly wages are $1650 for employees injured from 12/31/87 to 6/30/89. Increased to $1800 per month on 7/1/89 and $2100 on 7/1/91.

Ark. *Increased to $209.08 for deaths on or after 1/1/89.
**Benefits in excess of $75,000 payable from Death and Permanent Total Disability Trust Fund.

Colo. *Maximum is 80% of SAWW; minimum is 25% of maximum.
**Social Security offset.

Conn. *Maximum is 150% of SAWW and minimum is 20% of maximum (80% of average weekly wages if less). Employer funded cost of living increase payable each October.

Del. *Maximum is 80% of SAWW for spouse and children, 66-2/3% of SAWW for spouse only. Minimum for spouse only is 1/3 of maximum for spouse only.
**Additional burial allowance payable on Board approval.

D.C. *Maximum is 100% of SAWW (but not less than $513.00); minimum is 25% of SAWW or 80% of actual earnings, if less. Social Security offset.

Fla. *Maximum is 100% of SAWW. Surviving spouse entitled to tuition benefits at vocational-technical center or community college.

Ga. *Weekly benefits increased 20%, not to exceed $20,000, if death of employee was direct result of injury caused by intentional act of employer.

Guam *Spouse 35% and each child thereafter 15% of AWW, total not to exceed 66⅔% of AWW.
**Actual wages if less.

Hawaii *Maximum is 100% of SAWW for spouse and children, 75% of SAWW for spouse only. Minimum is 25% of SAWW.
**Maximum amount for persons other than spouse and children is the maximum benefit times 312.
***Funeral expense is 10 times SAWW, plus burial allowance equal to 5 times SAWW.

Idaho *Death benefit is fixed at 45% of SAWW for spouse plus 5% of SAWW per dependent child up to 3; 30% of SAWW for one child if no dependent spouse.

Ill. *Maximum is 133-1/3% of SAWW; minimum is 50% of SAWW.
**Benefits are $250,000 or 20 years at TT rate, whichever is greater. Child under 18 is entitled to at least 6 years' benefits.

Ind. *Effective 7/1/88.

Iowa *Maximum is 200% of SAWW.

Kan. *Maximum is 75% of SAWW.

Ky. *Maximum is 75% of SAWW for spouse and children, 50% of SAWW for spouse only. Minimum is 20% of SAWW.

La. *Maximum is 75% of SAWW. Minimum is 20% of SAWW, actual wage if less.

Maine *Maximum frozen at $447.92 until 7/1/89.
**Minimum does not apply to handicapped person employed by sheltered workshop at time of fatal injury.

Md. *Maximum is 100% of SAWW.
**Additional burial allowance payable on Commission approval.

Mass. *Maximum is 100% of SAWW. Annual cost of living increase payable up to 5% for deaths after that date.
**After receiving an amount equal to 250 times SAWW, spouse must prove actual dependence; time and amount limits do not apply to children's benefits.

Mich. *Maximum is 90% of SAWW, minimum is 50% of SAWW.
**500-week limit does not apply to children.

Minn. *Maximum is 100% of SAWW.
**Government survivors' benefits offset. During dependency of children; then 10 years' benefits.
***For unrelated death while decedent was receiving permanent partial disability, impairment compensation or economic recovery compensation benefits, benefits continue to surviving spouse and children until completed or until 10 years after dependency, whichever is earlier.

Miss. *Effective 7/1/88.

Mo. *Maximum is 75% of SAWW, effective 9/28/86.
**4 years' benefits payable to child on active duty in armed forces at age 18 who enrolls in school prior to age 23.

Mont. *Maximum is 100% of SAWW; minimum is 50% of SAWW, actual wage if less.

Nev. *Maximum is 100% of SAWW.

N.H. *Maximum is 150% of SAWW; minimum is 40% of SAWW or actual wages if less.
**On remarriage, the unpaid balance otherwise due is payable to parent or guardian for the children's benefit.

N.J. *Maximum is 75% of SAWW; minimum is 20% of SAWW.
**After 450 weeks, spouse's earnings are deducted.

N.M. *Maximum is 85% SAWW.

N.Y. *Social Security offset.
**Effective 7/1/85.

CHART VIII ☐ FATALITIES—INCOME BENEFITS FOR SPOUSE AND CHILDREN ☐ January 1, 1989 (continued)

JURISDICTION	PERCENT OF WAGES			MAXIMUM WEEKLY PAYMENT		MINIMUM PER WEEK SPOUSE ONLY	TIME LIMIT	AMOUNT LIMIT[1]		MAXIMUM BURIAL ALLOWANCE
	SPOUSE PLUS CHILDREN	SPOUSE ONLY	ONE CHILD ONLY	SPOUSE PLUS CHILDREN	SPOUSE ONLY			SPOUSE PLUS CHILDREN	SPOUSE ONLY	
NORTH CAROLINA	66-2/3	66-2/3	66-2/3	$ 376.00*	$ 376.00*	$30.00	(2,3,**)			$2,000
NORTH DAKOTA[9]	66-2/3*	66-2/3	66-2/3	(•)	210.00	105.00	(2)	(•)	$197,000	2,500
OHIO	66-2/3	66-2/3	66-2/3	400.00*	400.00*	200.00*	(2,4)			3,200
OKLAHOMA[9]	66-2/3	50	35	231.00*	173.58*	30.00[8]	(2,4)			1,000[10]
OREGON				494.60*	247.32*	247.32*	(2,6)			3,000
PENNSYLVANIA	66-2/3	51	32	399.00*	399.00*	199.50*	(2,4)			1,500
PUERTO RICO	85	50	60	46.15*	36.92*	17.30*	(2,4,**)			600
RHODE ISLAND	80	66-2/3	66-2/3	(•)	360.00*		(2,3)			5,000
SOUTH CAROLINA	66-2/3	66-2/3	66-2/3	334.87*	334.87*	25.00	500 weeks[2]	*167,435*	*167,435*	2,500
SOUTH DAKOTA	66-2/3	66-2/3	66-2/3	(•)	281.00*	141.00*	(2,4)			3,000[7]
TENNESSEE	66-2/3	50	50	231.00*	231.00*	25.00*	(2,3)	75,600*	75,600*	3,000**
TEXAS	66-2/3	66-2/3	66-2/3	238.00	238.00	39.00	(2,4)			2,500
UTAH	66-2/3*	66-2/3	66-2/3	292.00*	292.00*	45.00[8]	(2,**)			1,800
VERMONT	76-2/3	66-2/3	71-2/3	514.00*	514.00*	171.00*	(2,**)			2,000
VIRGIN ISLANDS				(•)	(•)	(•)	(2)	16,500*	16,500*	800[10]
VIRGINIA	66-2/3	66-2/3	66-2/3	362.00*	362.00*	90.50*	500 weeks[2]	*181,000*	*181,000*	3,000[7]
WASHINGTON[9]	70	60	35	384.26*	384.26*	43.02	(2,6)			2,000
WEST VIRGINIA	70	70	70	358.52*	358.52*	119.51*	(2,3)			3,500
WISCONSIN	66-2/3	66-2/3	66-2/3	363.00*	363.00*	30.00	(**)	*108,900****	*108,900****	1,500
WYOMING				(•)	237.47*	237.47*	(•)	(•)	(•)	1,800**
F.E.C.A.	75*	50	40	1,071.68	1,071.68	165.63	(2,4,**)			800[7,***]
LONGSHORE ACT	66-2/3	50	50	636.24*	636.24*	159.06*	(2,4)			3,000

N.C. *Maximum is 100% of SAWW.
**Payable for life if spouse disabled at time of decedent's death.

N.C. *Maximum is 110% of SAWW.

N.D. *Maximum $210 plus $7 per dependent child under 18 or 22 if in school. Payments on behalf of children are not subject to amount limit; minimum 50% of maximum weekly death benefit. Effective 7/1/85, claimants receiving death benefits between 7/1/80 and 7/1/85 are eligible for supplemental benefits not less than $90 per week.

Ohio *Maximum is 100% of SAWW; minimum is 50% of SAWW.

Okla. *Maximum is 66-2/3% of SAWW.

Ore. *Monthly spousal benefit is fixed at 66-2/3% of SAWW x 4.35 for spouse with no children ($1,075.66 for 1988-89) and fixed at 50% of SAWW x 4.35 for spouse with children ($806.83 for 1988-89), up to monthly maximum; maximum is 133-1/3% of SAWW x 4.35 ($2,151.51 for 1988-89). Upon remarriage, surviving spouse receives 24 times the monthly benefit in lump sum final payment.

Pa. *Maximum is 100% of SAWW; minimum is 50% of SAWW.

P.R. *Maximum for spouse and children is $200 monthly; for spouse only, $160 monthly. Minimum is $75 monthly.
**540-week limit inapplicable to spouse and children.

R.I. *Maximum is 100% of SAWW plus $15 per dependent child. Annual cost of living increase of 4% on anniversary.

S.C. *Maximum is 100% of SAWW.

S.D. *Maximum is 100% of SAWW; minimum is 50% of SAWW, actual wage if less. Additional $50 monthly is payable for each dependent child through age 18.

Tenn. *Effective 7/1/87.
**Employer must pay $10,000 lump sum into estate if worker had no dependents.

Utah *Additional allowance for dependents is $5 for spouse plus $5 for dependent child (up to 4). Maximum (including dependents' allowance) is 85% of SAWW.
**After 312 weeks payments are continued only after annual review. Receives same payment minus 50% Social Security payment. Balance of 312 weeks or 52 weeks is payable to spouse upon remarriage, whichever less.

Vt. *Maximum is 150% of SAWW; minimum is 50% of SAWW, actual wage if less.
**To spouse until age 62 or when entitled to Social Security; balance of 330 weeks, if any, is payable on remarriage.

V.I. *Death benefit is $12,500 to $16,500, payable in installments or lump sum; 60% is payable to children, if any. Amount limit includes amounts paid for disability.

Va. *Maximum is 100% of SAWW; minimum is 25% of SAWW, actual wage if less.

Wash. *Maximum monthly benefit is 100% of state average monthly wage ($1,652.33 for deaths occurring from 7/1/88 to 6/30/89 or $19,828 annually).

W. Va. *Maximum is 100% of SAWW; minimum is 33-1/3% of SAWW.

Wis. *Maximum is 100% of SAWW. Benefits are payable on monthly basis.
**If death follows disability, total time limit for disability plus death is 1,000 weeks.
***Amount limit is 300 times SAWW. When primary benefit expires, a supplementary monthly benefit continues for children at 10% of the spouse's monthly benefit, payable from the Children's Fund, to age 18 or for 15 years if invalid.

Wyo. *Monthly benefit is fixed at 66-2/3% of state average monthly wage plus $100 monthly per child until age 19 (21 if invalid or emancipated). After 54 months, hearing examiner may continue payments at 33-1/3% of state average monthly wage for 12 months and may be renewed.
**Employer may make other arrangements.

F.E.C.A. *2 or more children.
**Spouse who remarries after age 60 continues to receive monthly benefits.
***Additional $200 lump sum payable for cost of terminating status as U.S. employee.

Longshore *Effective 10/1/88 (200% NAWW). Benefits shall not exceed lesser of employee's weekly wage or $636.24. Minimum is 50% of NAWW, actual wages if less. Death benefits not payable if employee receiving PP benefits dies from causes other than compensable injury.

APPENDIX E
INCOME BENEFITS FOR SCHEDULED INJURIES*

* Source: U.S. CHAMBER OF COMMERCE, 1989 ANALYSIS OF WORKERS' COMPENSATION LAWS, "Chart VII, Income Benefits for Scheduled Injuries, January 1, 1989," pp. 22–23.

CHART VII INCOME BENEFITS FOR SCHEDULED INJURIES January 1, 1989

JURISDICTION	ARM AT SHOULDER	HAND	THUMB	FIRST FINGER	SECOND FINGER	THIRD FINGER	FOURTH FINGER	LEG AT HIP	FOOT	GREAT TOE	OTHER TOES	ONE EYE	HEARING ONE EAR	HEARING BOTH EARS
IN THIS GROUP OF STATES, COMPENSATION FOR TEMPORARY DISABILITY IS ALLOWED IN ADDITION TO ALLOWANCE FOR SCHEDULED INJURY														
ALABAMA*	$48,840	$37,400	$13,640	$ 9,460	$ 6,820	$ 4,840	$ 3,520	$44,000	$30,580	$ 7,040	$ 2,420	$27,280	$11,660	$35,860
ALASKA*	No schedule. Benefits paid according to degree of impairment.*													
AMERICAN SAMOA	PPD benefits paid at 66-2/3% of wages for specified number of weeks, no maximum.*													
ARIZONA*	*54,450*	*45,375*	13,613	8,168	6,353	4,538	3,630	45,375	36,300	6,353	2,269	*27,225*	18,150	54,450
ARKANSAS*	32,930	24,776	9,879	5,802	5,018	3,293	2,509	28,853	20,542	5,018	1,725	16,465	6,586	24,776
CALIFORNIA*	*58,975***	43,540	7,595	3,360	3,360	2,520	2,520	64,575**	33,740	4,235	840	21,105**	6,335	43,540
COLORADO*	31,200	15,600	7,500	3,900	2,700	1,650	1,950	31,200	15,600	3,900	1,650	20,850	5,250	20,850
CONNECTICUT*	*209,352*	*169,092*	*63,745*	36,234	29,524	20,801	17,446	159,698	126,148	28,182	8,723	157,685	34,892	104,676
DELAWARE	66,285	58,331	19,886	13,257	10,606	7,954	5,303	66,285	42,422	10,606	3,977	53,028	19,886	46,400
DISTRICT OF COLUMBIA	160,056	125,172	38,475	23,598	15,390	12,825	7,695	147,744	105,165	15,390	8,208	82,080	26,676	102,600
FLORIDA	No schedule. Benefits paid according to degree of impairment and loss of earnings.*													
GEORGIA	39,375	28,000	10,500	7,000	6,125	5,250	4,375	39,375	23,625	5,250	3,500	26,250	13,125	26,250
GUAM	39,200	29,680	7,140	3,920	2,520	2,380	980	34,720	24,220	3,640	1,120	19,600	7,280	28,000
HAWAII*	111,696	87,352	26,850	16,468	10,740	8,950	5,370	103,104	73,390	13,604	5,728	*57,280*	18,616	71,600
IDAHO*	53,295	47,966	19,542	12,436	9,771	4,441	2,665	35,530	24,871	7,461	1,244	*31,089*	—	31,089
ILLINOIS*	136,509	110,369	40,662	23,236	20,331	14,522	11,618	116,178	90,038	20,331	6,971	*87,134*	29,045	116,178
IOWA*	151,750	115,330	36,420	21,245	18,210	15,175	12,140	133,540	91,050	24,280	9,105	84,980	30,350	106,225
MAINE*	No schedule. Benefits paid according to degree of impairment.													
MARYLAND*	122,400	101,898	13,600	3,300	2,888	2,475	2,063	122,400	101,898	3,300	825	101,898	17,000	101,898
MASSACHUSETTS*	*19,101*	*15,103*	—	—	—	—	—	17,324	12,882	—	—	17,324	12,882	34,203
MINNESOTA	No schedule. Benefits paid according to degree of impairment and loss of earnings.*													
MISSISSIPPI	39,600	29,700	11,880	6,930	5,940	3,960	2,970	34,650	24,750	5,940	1,980	19,800	7,920	29,700
MISSOURI*	38,925	29,362	10,067	7,550	5,872	5,872	3,691	*34,730*	26,006	6,711	2,349	23,489	7,382	28,187
MONTANA*	No schedule. Benefits paid according to degree of impairment and loss of earnings.*													
NEBRASKA*	55,125	42,875	14,700	8,575	7,350	4,900	3,675	52,675	36,750	7,350	2,450	30,625	12,250	(**)
NEVADA	No schedule. Degree of disability determined in relation to whole man.*													
NEW HAMPSHIRE	117,495	105,746	42,522	26,297	21,261	10,631	5,036	78,330	54,831	10,071	1,679	46,998	16,785	68,819
NEW JERSEY*	82,764	50,274	6,840	4,560	3,648	2,736	1,824	79,002	41,952	3,648	1,368	40,128	5,472	31,920

NEW MEXICO	*56,740*	*35,463*	15,604	7,944	6,241	4,823	3,972	*56,740*	32,626	9,930	3,972	36,881	11,348	42,555
NORTH CAROLINA	90,240	75,200	28,200	16,920	15,040	9,400	7,520	75,200	54,144	13,160	3,760	45,120	26,320	56,400
NORTH DAKOTA*	*18,750*	*15,000*	*4,875*	*3,000*	*2,250*	*1,500*	*1,200*	14,040	9,000	1,800	720	9,000	3,000	12,000
OHIO*	90,000	70,000	24,000	14,000	12,000	8,000	6,000	80,000	60,000	12,000	4,000	50,000	10,000	50,000
OREGON*	27,840	21,750	6,960	3,480	3,190	1,450	870	21,750	19,575	2,610	580	14,500	8,700	27,840
PUERTO RICO*	12,000	12,000	4,875	2,600	1,950	1,625	1,300	12,000	11,375	1,950	975	(**)	3,250	12,000
RHODE ISLAND*	28,080	21,960	6,750	4,140	2,700	2,250	1,800	28,080	18,450	3,420	900	14,400	5,400	18,000
SOUTH CAROLINA	73,671	61,951	21,767	13,395	11,720	8,372	6,697	65,300	46,882	11,720	3,349	46,882	26,790	55,254
SOUTH DAKOTA	56,200	42,150	14,050	9,835	8,430	5,620	4,215	44,960	35,125	8,430	2,810	42,150	14,050	42,150
TENNESSEE	46,200	34,650	13,860	8,085	6,930	4,620	3,465	46,200	28,875	6,930	2,310	23,100	17,325	34,650
UTAH*	42,823	38,472	15,343	9,618	7,786	3,893	1,832	28,625	20,152	5,954	916	*27,480*	3,815	22,900
VERMONT*	110,510	89,950	25,700	16,448	12,850	10,280	6,168	110,510	89,950	12,850	5,140	64,250	26,728	110,510
VIRGINIA*	72,400	54,300	21,720	12,670	10,860	7,240	5,430	63,350	45,250	10,860	3,620	36,200	18,100	36,200
VIRGIN ISLANDS*	40,260	32,940	14,640	14,640	14,640	14,640	13,725	32,940	21,960	14,640	13,725**	35,685	21,960	32,940
WASHINGTON*	54,000	48,600	19,440	12,150	9,720	4,860	2,430	54,000	37,800	11,340	4,140	21,600	7,200	43,200
WEST VIRGINIA*	57,362	47,802	19,121	9,560	6,692	4,780	4,780	57,362	33,461	9,560	3,824	31,549	21,511	52,582
WISCONSIN*	62,500	50,000	20,000	7,500	5,625	3,250	3,500	62,500	31,250	10,416	3,125**	*34,375*	6,875	41,250***
WYOMING*	8,311	6,887	2,612	1,662	950	950	950	7,599	5,699	1,187	475	5,699	2,850	5,699
F.E.C.A.*	334,364	261,490	80,376	49,297	32,150	26,792	16,075	308,644	219,694	40,724	17,147	171,469	55,727	214,336
LONGSHORE ACT	198,507	155,243	47,718	29,267	19,087	15,906	9,544	183,237	130,429	19,087	10,180	101,798	33,084	127,248
IN THIS GROUP OF STATES, COMPENSATION FOR TEMPORARY DISABILITY IS ALLOWED IN ADDITION TO SCHEDULED INJURY WITH CERTAIN LIMITATIONS AS TO PERIOD														
INDIANA*	41,500	33,200	9,960	6,640	5,810	4,980	3,320	37,350	29,050	9,960	4,980	29,050	12,450	33,200
KANSAS*	55,230	39,450	15,780	9,731	7,890	5,260	3,945	52,600	32,875	7,890	2,630	31,560	7,890	28,930
NEW YORK*	93,600	73,200	22,500	13,800	9,000	7,500	4,500	86,400	61,500	11,400	4,800	48,000	18,000	45,000
PENNSYLVANIA*	163,590	133,665	39,900	19,950	15,960	11,970	11,172	163,590	99,750	15,960	6,384	109,725	23,940	103,740
IN THIS GROUP OF STATES, COMPENSATION FOR TEMPORARY DISABILITY IS DEDUCTED FROM THE ALLOWANCE FOR SCHEDULED INJURY														
KENTUCKY	No schedule. PP benefits paid at 66-2/3% of wages up to 425 weeks according to degree of disability.*,**													
LOUISIANA*	53,400	40,050	13,350	8,010	5,340	5,340	5,340	46,725	33,375	5,340	2,670	26,700	—	26,700**
MICHIGAN*	110,021	87,935	26,585	15,542	13,497	8,998	6,544	87,935	66,258	13,497	4,499	66,258	(**)	(**)
OKLAHOMA*	43,250	34,600	10,380	6,055	5,190	3,460	2,595	43,250	34,600	5,190	1,730	34,600	17,300	51,900
TEXAS	47,600	35,700	14,280	10,710	7,140	4,998	3,570	47,600	29,750	7,140	2,380	23,800	—	35,700

NOTE—Amounts in chart reflect maximum potential entitlement. In Canada, permanent physical impairments generally are compensated by degree of disability using medical rating schedules as guidelines. Numbers in italics are computations for loss of major member, loss of leg precluding use of artificial limb, or loss of eye by enucleation.

(See following page for chart footnotes.)

Ala. Maximum weekly PP benefit is lesser of $220 or 100% SAWW.

Alaska *Compensation is $135,000 multiplied by the employee's percentage of permanent impairment based on the *AMA Guide to the Evaluation of Permanent Impairment*.

Am. Samoa *Arm—312, hand—244, thumb—75, first finger—46, second finger—30, third finger—25, fourth finger—15, leg—288, foot—205, great toe—30, other toes—16, one eye—160, one ear—52, both ears—200.

Ariz. *PP benefit is 55% of maximum monthly compensation.

Ark. *PP benefit is 66-2/3% of employee's average weekly wages; maximum is $156.81 per week, minimum is $20 per week. Maximum amount for PP is $75,000.

Calif. *Maximum PP benefit is $140.00, effective 1/1/84. Duration varies according to percentage of permanent disability, adjusted for age and occupation. Chart reflects standard rating for individual age 39 and loss of major arm.
**Chart reflects benefits for loss of eye if unable to wear artificial eye. Life pension up to $64.21 weekly also payable for loss of arm or leg.

Colo. *Maximum weekly benefit is $150. The weekly rate for a "working unit" award is $120; maximum award is $37,560.

Conn. *Commission may award additional benefits based on loss of earnings.

Fla. *Permanent impairment caused by amputation, loss of 80% of vision in either eye after correction, or serious facial disfigurement—$250 per 1% of disability up to 10%, and $500 per 1% of disability over 10%. Wage-loss benefits also payable in all permanent impairment cases—95% of difference between 85% of pre-injury wages and earnings after maximum medical improvement, up to 100% of SAWW weekly; Social Security retirement benefits are deducted from wage loss benefits.

Hawaii *In cases in which the disability is determined as a percentage of total loss or impairment of physical or mental function of the whole man, the maximum compensation is the corresponding percentage of 312 times SAWW ($111,696 effective 1/1/89).

Idaho *Maximum weekly PP benefit is 55% of SAWW for year in which injury occurred ($177.65 for 1989).

Ill. *Effective January 15. Figures reflect benefits for amputation of member—maximum 133-1/3% of SAWW ($580.89 as of 1/15/89). For other PP benefits, wage replacement rate is 60% and maximum is $302.44.

Ind. *Payable for 78 weeks; maximum weekly PP benefit is $166 (increased to $183 on 7/1/89 and to $200 on 7/1/90.).
**Second toe—$4,980, third toe—$3,320, fourth toe—$2,490, fifth toe—$1,660.

Iowa *Maximum weekly PP benefit is 184% of SAWW (= $607.00).

Kan. *Additional healing period up to 15 weeks may be allowed. Maximum weekly PP benefit is 75% of SAWW.

Ky. *Maximum weekly PP benefit is 75% of SAWW. Degree of disability is determined by American Medical Association Guide or decrease in earning capacity, whichever is greater.
**Since 1980, an employee sustaining work-related hearing loss is entitled to either functional loss to the body as a whole or occupational disability, whichever is greater. Hearing loss claims receive same treatment as occupational diseases and injuries, with a final determination by the Board as to degree of disability.

La. *Schedule applies to amputation or disability greater than 25%. Supplemental earnings benefits are 66-2/3% of the difference between 90% of pre-injury wages and post-injury earnings, maximum 520 weeks; cease 2 years after termination of temporary total disability (unless paid for 13 consecutive weeks during that time) or upon retirement or receipt of Social Security retirement benefits.
**Permanent hearing loss due to single traumatic accident.

Maine *For injuries on or after 11/20/87, the *AMA Guide to the Evaluation of Permanent Impairment* will be used until Commission adopts, by rule, a schedule. No petition for permanent impairment may be filed until the employee reaches maximum medical improvement.

Md. *Maximum weekly PP benefit is $82.50 where benefits are payable for less than 75 weeks; 33-1/3% of SAWW ($136.00) where benefits are payable for 75 weeks but less than 250 weeks; and 75% SAWW ($306.00) where benefits are payable for 250 or more weeks.

Mass. *Maximum PP benefit is 100% of SAWW (= $444.20). Proportional benefits for partial loss of limbs (fingers, toes).

Mich. *Wage-loss benefits payable for life.
**Hearing loss compensable based on lost earnings.

Minn. *For permanent partial disability, impairment compensation (IC) is paid in lump sum if take job. If no job offer made, economic recovery compensation (ER) is paid weekly. IC equals scheduled dollar amount ($75,000 to $400,000) times percent whole body disability. ER equals percent disability times scheduled number of weeks (600 to 1200 weeks) times weekly TT rate. Concurrent payment of PPD and temporary benefits allowed in certain situations.

Mo. *Maximum weekly PP benefit is 45% of SAWW ($167.78 effective 7/1/88); minimum is $40. If amputation or 100% loss of use, additional 10% compensation.
**Occupational hearing loss law provides benefits up to 40 weeks (1 ear) or 148 weeks (both ears).

Mont. *For injuries on or after 7/1/87, benefits are paid according to degree of impairment and a wage supplement rate, which is 2/3 of the difference between wages actually received at time of injury and wage worker is qualified to earn in a local or state-wide job pool. The maximum partial disability benefit is 50% SAWW and terminates on receipt of or eligibility for Social Security retirement.

Neb. *Terms run consecutively for loss of, or loss of use of, more than 1 member but less than total disability.
**Permanent total loss of hearing is compensated as permanent total disability.

Nev. *Each 1% of impairment is compensated by .6% of worker's monthly wage up to maximum, payable for 5 years or until age 70, whichever is later. Maximum monthly wages are $2,395.49 as of 7/1/88.

N.J. *Computations include allowance for amputation of member (30% additional compensation). Compensation is payable weekly at 70% of pre-injury weekly wages, up to a maximum of 55% of SAWW for arm or leg, 45% of SAWW for hand, 40% of SAWW for foot or one eye, 35% of SAWW for hearing—both ears, 20% of SAWW for other scheduled injuries in chart.

N.Y. *Additional weeks for TT in excess of statutory healing period; maximum $150 as of 7/1/85. Compensation for wage-loss in addition to schedule if impairment due to loss of 50% or more of member.

N.C. *For unscheduled injuries, maximum compensation not to exceed $20,000.

N.D. *PP benefit is $60 weekly for scheduled number of weeks; amount includes 25% additional for master hand.

Ohio *Maximum weekly PP benefit is 100% of SAWW (= $400.00 for 1989). Compensation payable for 200 weeks if percentage of disability is 90% or greater.

Okla. *Maximum PP benefit is 50% of SAWW (= $173.00 effective 11/1/87).

Ore. *Calculated at $145 per degree for scheduled injury; $100 per degree for unscheduled injury with a maximum of 320 degrees.

Pa. *Healing period is 25 weeks for leg or foot; 20 weeks for an arm or hand; 12 weeks for great toe; 10 weeks for thumb, eye, or hearing; 6 weeks for finger or toe.

P.R. *Maximum PP benefit is $65 weekly. Maximum amount for PPD is $12,000.
**Permanent visual disability is compensated according to percentage of total disability; in addition, loss of eye by enucleation is compensated at 10% of permanent total disability.

R.I. *Maximum scheduled PP benefit is $90.00 weekly. Maximum is 100% of SAWW for unscheduled injury.

Utah *Maximum per week, including allowance for dependents, is 66-2/3% of SAWW (= $229 effective 7/1/88).
**Entry presumes total loss of hearing in one ear and no loss of hearing in the other (16-2/3 weeks).

Vt. *In addition to TT except for loss of hearing in 1 ear.

Va. *Benefits for scheduled injuries are payable in addition to compensation for temporary disability. *County of Spotsylvania v. Hart*, 218 Va. 565, 238 S.E.2d 813 (1977). TTD payments continue until claimant is released to return to work at which time award for specific disability may be entered and paid simultaneously with payment for temporary partial benefits.

V.I. *PP benefit is 66-2/3% of SAWW weekly (= $183.00 effective 1/1/85).
**For loss of two or more digits or one or more phalanges of two or more digits on a hand or foot, benefits may be proportioned to the loss of use of the hand or foot.

Wash. *Benefits fixed at amount reflected in chart.

W.Va. *Maximum weekly benefit is 66-2/3% SAWW (= $239.01 effective 7/1/88).

Wis. *Maximum weekly PP benefit is $125 effective 1/1/89.
**Second toe and other toes—$2,500.
***Under occupational hearing loss law, maximum is $4,500/36 weeks for one ear and $27,000/216 weeks for both ears, as of 1/1/89.

Wyo. *PP benefit is 66-2/3% of SAMW for specified months according to degree of impairment (= $1,029.04 as of 1/1/89).

F.E.C.A. *Includes allowance for dependents.

APPENDIX F
Rehabilitation of Disabled Workers*

* Source: U.S. Chamber of Commerce, 1989 Analysis of Workers' Compensation Laws, "Chart X, Rehabilitation of Disabled Workers, January 1, 1989," pp. 28–29.

CHART X REHABILITATION OF DISABLED WORKERS January 1, 1989

JURISDICTION	SOURCE OF FUND	MAINTENANCE ALLOWANCE	SPECIAL PROVISIONS
ALABAMA	No fund established	Board, lodging, and travel, if away from home.	Physical and vocational rehabilitation to restore employee to gainful employment furnished at employer's expense. Employee's refusal results in loss of compensation.
ALASKA	No fund established	Board, lodging, travel, and temporary disability benefits.	Employer pays full cost, on an expense incurred basis, not to exceed $10,000. Benefits may not extend past two years from date of reemployment plan approval. Compensation suspended for unreasonable refusal of evaluation or failure to participate in approved or agreed plan.
AMERICAN SAMOA	Second Injury Fund	$10 weekly paid by employer plus maintenance from Special Fund.	Commission arranges for vocational rehabilitation of permanently disabled workers.
ARIZONA	Appropriations annually from general fund up to 2% of annual premium.	Commission may authorize additional necessary awards to persons undergoing vocational rehabilitation.	Vocational rehabilitation trainees considered an employee at $200 monthly wage rate for compensation benefits.
ARKANSAS	No fund established	Reasonable expenses for maintenance, travel, and other necessary costs for 60 weeks maximum.	Must apply to Commission. Commission may authorize vocational rehabilitation if reasonable in relation to disability, but worker may refuse.
CALIFORNIA	No fund established	All additional necessary living expenses during rehabilitation.	Rehabilitation unit in Division of Industrial Accidents. Rehabilitation program is compulsory on part of employer or carrier. Rehabilitation trainee is considered employee of training employer for insurance purposes.
COLORADO	No fund established for vocational rehabilitation	Maintenance, tuition, and transportation during 26 weeks.	Period of time may be extended another 26 weeks if necessary. Employee cannot receive disability benefits and maintenance simultaneously. If totally disabled employee refuses suitable employment or vocational rehabilitation, PT benefits will not be awarded.*
CONNECTICUT	2% tax upon compensation paid by insurers and self-insurers	Weekly subsistence allowance during vocational rehabilitation.	Employer pays full cost of medical rehabilitation, which continues until employee reaches maximum improvement. Vocational rehabilitation is furnished by Division of Workers' Rehabilitation.
DELAWARE	No fund established	Reasonable board, lodging, and travel.	Physical and vocational rehabilitation furnished at employer's expense. Employee's refusal results in loss of compensation.
DISTRICT OF COLUMBIA	No fund established	Not exceeding $50 per week.	Employer must provide vocational rehabilitation. Benefits forfeited if worker fails to cooperate.
FLORIDA	Payments from Special Fund and assessments upon insurers and self-insurers	Reasonable board, lodging, and travel.	Injured worker is entitled to prompt rehabilitation including retraining, provided by or at the expense of the employer. Rehabilitation may be up to 26 weeks extendable for an additional 26 weeks. Refusal to accept rehabilitation deemed necessary by deputy commissioner results in automatic 50% reduction in compensation for each week of refusal.
GEORGIA	No fund established	Reasonable board, lodging, and travel, if away from home.	Vocational rehabilitation furnished for 26 weeks but may be extended if necessary. Employee's unreasonable refusal may result in suspension of compensation.
GUAM	State fund (appropriation)	$10 per week during retraining.	Commission directs the vocational rehabilitation of permanently disabled employees and arranges with the appropriate public or private agencies for such education.
HAWAII	No fund established	Board, lodging, travel, tuition, books, and basic materials in addition to compensation.	Rehabilitation unit within Department of Labor and Industrial Relations makes recommendation for physical or vocational rehabilitation. Director approves services and reviews progress.
IDAHO	.7% tax on insurers and self-insurers	Reasonable expenses for maintenance and travel.	Rehabilitation Division administers. Temporary disability benefits payable up to 104 weeks where retraining required.
ILLINOIS	No fund established	Maintenance costs and incidental expenses.	Physical, mental, and vocational rehabilitation as may be necessary. Institutional care, if required.
INDIANA	No fund established	No specific statutory provision*	

IOWA	No fund established	$20 weekly in addition to other compensation for 13 weeks.	May be extended additional 13 weeks. Medical care includes physical rehabilitation.
KANSAS	No fund established	Employer must pay reasonable board, lodging, and travel up to $3,500 for a 26-week period (may be increased to $5,500).	Employer or carrier must refer certain employees to an approved rehabilitation vendor for vocational evaluation. Employer must provide up to 36 weeks (may be extended an additional 36 weeks). Disability payments suspended for worker's refusal to participate in rehabilitation. After 90 days refusal, Director may reduce compensation to not less than PPD payments.
KENTUCKY	No fund established	Board, lodging, and travel, if away from home.	Unlimited medical rehabilitation; vocational rehabilitation up to 52 weeks (may be extended). Employee's refusal results in loss of 50% of compensation.
LOUISIANA	No fund established	Board, lodging, and travel paid by employer or carrier.	Employer or carrier provides up to 26 weeks of vocational rehabilitation, extendable another 26 weeks. Benefits reduced 50% for refusal of necessary rehabilitation.
MAINE	Employment Rehabilitation Fund*	Tuition, books, fees, and sum for sustenance and travel not to exceed 25% of SAWW. Employees injured before 6/30/85 may receive additional $35 weekly.	Office of Employment Rehabilitation monitors cases. Employer must file report within 120 days of injury if employee has not returned to employment. Benefits suspended if employee does not comply with program. Commission may order mandatory retraining of employees injured on or after 11/20/87.
MARYLAND	No fund established	Up to $40 weekly paid by employer.	Workmen's Compensation Commission investigates all claims and reports of injury or disability for referral to Division of Vocational Rehabilitation. Employee entitled to 24 months of vocational rehabilitation. Employee's unreasonable refusal results in loss of compensation. Employer pays compensation for temporary total disability plus expenses of vocational assessment and rehabilitation.
MASSACHUSETTS	No fund established. Paid the same as compensation by employer or insurer.	Office of Education and Vocational Rehabilitation may approve room, board, and travel expenses for 52 weeks.	Necessary cost of rehabilitation subject to approval of Office of Education and Vocational Rehabilitation. Benefits suspended for refusal to participate.
MICHIGAN	No fund established	Transportation and other necessary expenses during 52 weeks training.	Medical and vocational rehabilitation services under Workers' Compensation Bureau—approved facility. Bureau may extend training period additional 52 weeks, maximum total 104 weeks.
MINNESOTA	No fund established.	Necessary expenses, including tuition, books, travel, board, lodging, and custodial daycare. Employee receives temporary total during approved retraining up to 156 weeks.	Qualified injured worker entitled to rehab. provided by/at expense of employer. If approved plan, employer to provide retraining up to 156 weeks.* Participant may request 25% benefit increase and is eligible for one-time relocation allowance. Employer may seek termination or suspension of benefits if worker fails to cooperate with plan.
MISSISSIPPI	No fund established	Up to $10 per week up to 52 weeks.	Commission cooperates with federal and state agencies.
MISSOURI	No fund established. At expense of employer or insurer.	$40 weekly for physical rehabilitation (by order of Division after 20 weeks).	Administered by Director of Worker's Compensation Division. Division may order employer to provide transportation.
MONTANA	Rehabilitation Fund by 1% tax upon compensation paid by insurers, self-insured, and state fund	Employee receives TT benefits up to 25 weeks from eligibility date. Up to $4,000 for travel and relocation expenses related to search for new employment or implementation of Division rehabilitation program.	Administered by Workers' Compensation Division rehabilitation panel. Services provided by private certified rehabilitation counselors. Employee also may be referred to the Department of Social and Rehabilitative Services. Employee's refusal may result in loss of compensation.
NEBRASKA	Vocational Rehabilitation Fund by 1% premium tax on insurers and self-insurers (minimum $25) payable to Court	Board, lodging, and travel paid by fund. Temporary indemnity paid by self-insurer or carrier.	Insurer must furnish medical, physical, and vocational rehabilitation services voluntarily (if not, may be ordered to do so). Costs may be apportioned between the employer and the Vocational Rehabilitation Fund. Payments into fund suspended when fund reaches $400,000 (see Chart XIII).
NEVADA	State Insurance Fund and self-insurance	Insurer may allow maintenance as needed.	Insurer is authorized to provide all necessary rehabilitation services. Employee's refusal results in loss of all benefits.
NEW HAMPSHIRE	No fund established	Board, lodging, travel, books, and basic materials in addition to compensation.	Insurer must furnish rehabilitation services voluntarily, or may be ordered to do so, for one year and further treatment if needed. Vocational and physical rehabilitation staff assist in program.
NEW JERSEY	No fund established		Permanent total disability benefits may be stopped after 450 weeks unless the worker has submitted to physical or educational retraining.

Colo. *Vocational rehabilitation is an optional benefit for injuries after July 2, 1987.
Ind. *State Rehabilitation Services Board administers vocational rehabilitation programs. Compensation suspended for refusal of suitable on employment by partially disabled claimant.
Maine *Funded by assessment of 0.5% on insurers and self-insurers in 1986 and 1.0% thereafter.
Minn. *Surviving spouse may request rehabilitation.

CHART X □ REHABILITATION OF DISABLED WORKERS □ January 1, 1989 (continued)

JURISDICTION	SOURCE OF FUND	MAINTENANCE ALLOWANCE	SPECIAL PROVISIONS
NEW MEXICO	No fund established	Board, lodging, tuition, travel and other expenses for up to two years.	The purpose of vocational rehabilitation is the restoration of the disabled worker to gainful employment, preferably that for which he has training or experience.
NEW YORK	$2,000 in no-dependency death cases	Up to $30 per week for rehabilitation maintenance.	Department of Labor cooperates with Department of Education.
NORTH CAROLINA	No fund established		Insurer must furnish rehabilitation services required to lessen disability. Employee's unreasonable refusal of services ordered by Commission results in loss of compensation.
NORTH DAKOTA	Benefit Fund	Rehabilitation allowance in lieu of and equal to compensation, plus 25%.	Bureau through its Director of Rehabilitation provides retraining. Employee's unreasonable refusal to cooperate shall forfeit compensation. Additional allowance of $10,000 maximum during lifetime, for remodeling living or business facilities, if required.
OHIO	State Insurance Fund	Same as for temporary total disability, minimum 50% of SAWW, for 6 months (renewable).*	Rehabilitation Division within Commission administers. Division may make all necessary expenditures, medically including treatment of non-occupational conditions inhibiting return to work.
OKLAHOMA	No fund established	Board, lodging, travel, tuition, and books.	Court may order necessary rehabilitation up to 52 weeks; may also order additional 52 weeks.
OREGON	No fund established	Worker receives temporary total disability compensation during rehabilitation.	Physical and vocational rehabilitation furnished at employers' expense and in accordance with Department regulations. Benefits may be suspended for failure to participate.
PENNSYLVANIA	No fund established	Rehabilitation Board may provide cash payments for living expenses.	State Board of Rehabilitation may provide vocational rehabilitation, training, and services.
PUERTO RICO	No fund established	Administrator may grant $45 weekly for up to 26 weeks.	Rehabilitation center provides physical, medical, and rehabilitation services.
RHODE ISLAND	$750 in no-dependency death cases; 1% of insurance premium	Board, lodging, and travel.	The Department operates the Dr. John E. Donley Rehabilitation Center. Compensation suspended for willful refusal of suitable employment or rehabilitation.
SOUTH CAROLINA	No fund established	No specific statutory provision	
SOUTH DAKOTA			TT during period of approved vocational rehabilitation.
TENNESSEE	No fund established		Division of Workers' Compensation refers feasible cases to Department of Education pursuant to plan providing full or partial recovery of expenses from employer or insurer.
TEXAS	No fund established		Insurer furnishes necessary medical care and services for physical rehabilitation. Board may refer employee to Texas Rehabilitation Commission for vocational services.
UTAH	$18,720 in no-dependency death cases	$1,000 maximum during rehabilitation of permanently and totally disabled person.	If cannot be rehabilitated, worker receives benefits for life from Second Injury Fund, minimum $120 per week.

VERMONT	No fund established	Board, lodging, travel, books, and tools.	Commissioner may order vocational rehabilitation services. If employee refuses, compensation may be suspended.
VIRGIN ISLANDS	Government Insurance Fund	Board, lodging, and travel.	Income benefits during rehabilitation suspended for employee's refusal to accept vocational rehabilitation. See Chart V—Total Disability Benefits.
VIRGINIA	Second Injury Fund		Commission may award compensation, medical care, and vocational rehabilitation. Employer may be required to furnish and maintain wheelchairs, bedside lifts, adjustable beds and make alterations to home, maximum $20,000. Employee's unreasonable refusal may suspend compensation.
WASHINGTON	No fund established	Compensation; board, lodging, travel, books, equipment, and child care allowance, up to 52 weeks (maximum $3,000).	Supervisor may extend period for another 52 weeks. Dept. operates a Rehabilitation Center and pays maintenance and employer's cost of job modification.
WEST VIRGINIA	State Fund used; no special account	Up to $10,000 (includes tuition, books, supplies, travel, lodging, and tools). No limit on physical rehabilitation costs. Temporary total disability payments if totally disabled.	Fund-employed Rehabilitation Counselors provide referrals and direct services. Direct job placement emphasized, but training considered on basis of need. Short term training preferred. Longer programs approved when no other employment alternatives available, normally limited to 2 years.
WISCONSIN	No fund established		40-week period may be extended with Division's permission if necessary. Division refers feasible cases to Department of Vocational Rehabilitation.
WYOMING	No fund established	Up to $10 per week (may be increased to $15 per week if insufficient) up to 72 weeks.	District judge grants maintenance allowance on recommendations of Board of Education.
F.E.C.A.	Employees' Compensation Fund	Up to $200 per month.	If person fails to undergo rehabilitation, administrator may reduce benefit if rehabilitation would have increased earnings.
LONGSHORE ACT	50% of Special Fund*	Up to $25 per week.	Surplus in Fund in any one year may be carried over. Appropriations authorized.

Ohio *If claimant returns to lesser-paying job while in rehabilitation, wage loss compensation of difference between wage at time of injury and wage at job while in rehabilitation program can be paid.

Longshore *See Chart XII—Second-Injury Funds—Special Provisions

APPENDIX G
SECOND-INJURY FUNDS*

* Source: U.S. CHAMBER OF COMMERCE, 1989 ANALYSIS OF WORKERS' COMPENSATION LAWS, "Chart XIII, Second-Injury Funds, January 1, 1989," pp. 38–41.

CHART XIII SECOND-INJURY FUNDS January 1, 1989

JURISDICTION	INJURIES COVERED	PAYABLE BY EMPLOYER	PAYABLE BY FUND	SOURCE OF FUND	SPECIAL PROVISIONS
ALABAMA	Second injury which combined with prior permanent partial disability results in permanent total disability.	Disability caused by second injury.	Difference between compensation payable for second injury and permanent total disability.	$100 in death cases	Employer must have knowledge of prior disabling injury affecting employability.
ALASKA	Second injury which added to pre-existing permanent physical impairment results in substantially greater disability than from second injury alone.	Disability caused by second injury up to 104 weeks.	Compensation in excess of 104 weeks.	Up to 6% of compensation payable to fund; percentage varies from 0% to 6% depending on fund balance. $10,000 in no-dependency death cases; civil penalties.	"Physical impairment" as listed or would support an award of 200 weeks or more.
AMERICAN SAMOA	Second injury which combined with prior permanent impairment results in death or compensable disability greater than from second injury alone.	Benefits for first 104 weeks.	Benefits beyond first 104 weeks.	$1,000 in no-dependency death cases, plus fines and penalties.	Employer must have prior knowledge of disability.
ARIZONA	Second injury which added to a pre-existing work-related disability or a pre-existing physical impairment not industrially related (25 types of handicaps as listed by statute) results in disability for work.	Disability caused by second injury.	Employer and special fund are equally liable for remaining difference between compensation payable for second injury and compensation for combined disability.	1.5% of all premiums and costs of self insurance. Commission may allocate up to .5% of yearly premiums to special fund to keep fund actuarially sound.	Employer must have knowledge of non-industrial physical impairment. Payments are also made from the fund for vocational rehabilitation, claims against non-insured employers, insolvent carriers, supportive medical care.
ARKANSAS	Second injury which added to previous permanent partial disability or impairment results in additional disability or impairment greater than from second injury alone.	Disability caused by second injury.	Difference between compensation payable for second injury and permanent disability.	$1,000 in no-dependency death cases. $500 to Second Injury Fund and $500 to Permanent Total Disability and Death Fund. Portion of premium tax.	Employer liable for combined disability of both injuries in same employment.
CALIFORNIA	Second permanent partial injury which added to pre-existing permanent partial disability results in 70 percent or more permanent disability. Second injury must account for 35 percent.*	Disability caused by second injury.	Difference between compensation payable for second injury and permanent disability.	Legislative appropriations and $50,000 in each no-dependency death case or unpaid balance.	Payments are made by State Compensation Insurance Fund.
COLORADO	Second injury which added to pre-existing permanent partial disability results in permanent total disability.	Disability caused by second injury.	Difference between compensation payable for second injury and permanent total disability.	$15,000 in no-dependency or partial-dependency cases, and tax of 4/10 of 1% of premiums received by insurance carriers and equivalent charge on self-insurers.	If employee obtains employment while receiving compensation from second-injury fund, fund compensates at rate of 1/2 of employee's average weekly wage loss during employment.
CONNECTICUT	Second injury or disease which added to pre-existing injury, disease, or congenital causes results in permanent disability greater than from second injury alone.	Benefits for first 104 weeks, less compensation payable for prior disability.	Benefits beyond first 104 weeks, less compensation payable for prior disability.*	Tax equal to 5% of compensation paid by carriers and self-insurers during preceding calendar year plus fines.	Tax imposed each time fund balance is reduced to $1,000,000.
DELAWARE	Second injury or disease which added to existing permanent injury from any cause results in permanent total disability.	Disability caused by second injury.	Difference between compensation payable for second injury and permanent disability.	Tax of 2% of premiums received by insurance carriers and equivalent charge on self-insurers.	Payments suspended when fund reaches $750,000 and resumed when below $250,000.

DISTRICT OF COLUMBIA	Second injury or disease which added to pre-existing injury, disease, or congenital causes results in permanent disability greater than from second injury alone.	Disability caused by second injury for first 104 weeks and first $1,000 medical expenses.	Difference between compensation payable for second injury and permanent disability.	$5,000 in no-dependency death cases or unpaid awards. Pro-rata assessments upon carriers and self-insurers based on paid losses. Fines and penalties.	
FLORIDA	Second injury or disease which merges with previous permanent physical impairment and results in substantially greater disability than from the second injury alone.		Fund reimburses employer for 60% of impairment benefits, 60% of wage-loss benefits during first 5 years after maximum medical improvements and 75% thereafter, PT benefits after 175 weeks, 75% of death benefits and funeral expenses, and 50% of first $10,000 in temporary disability and medical benefits and 100% beyond $10,000.	Prorata annual assessment upon net premiums of insurers and self-insurers.	Assessment must equal sum of immediate past 3 years' disbursements.
GEORGIA	Second injury or disease which merges with prior permanent physical impairment and results in greater disability than from second injury alone.	Disability caused by second injury for first 104 weeks.	Employer reimbursed for 50% of medical and rehabilitation expenses in excess of $5,000 up to $10,000, and 100% of medical and rehabilitation expenses in excess of $10,000, plus income benefits beyond 104 weeks.	Assessments on carriers and self-insurers proportionate to 175% of disbursements from fund to annual compensation benefits paid, less net assets in fund. In no-dependency death cases, 1/2 of benefits payable or $10,000, whichever is less.	Employer must have prior knowledge of impairment. Assessments may be reduced or suspended when no funds are needed.
GUAM	Second injury which combined with a previous disability causes permanent disability.	Disability caused by second injury.	Difference between compensation payable for second injury and compensable disability.	State fund (appropriation).	
HAWAII	Second injury which added to pre-existing disabilities results in greater permanent disability, permanent total disability, or death.	Disability benefits for first 104 weeks.	Benefits beyond first 104 weeks.	$8,775 in no-dependency death cases; and unpaid balance of compensation due in permanent total and permanent partial disability cases, if no dependents; 1/4% premium tax on insurers and self-insurers.	Premium tax suspended when balance exceeds $200,000, resumed when below $100,000.
IDAHO	Second injury which combined with prior permanent physical impairment results in permanent total disability.	Disability caused by second injury.	Difference between compensation payable for second injury and permanent disability.	Amount equal to 5% of all benefits except temporary disability income benefits and accrued medical benefits and $10,000 in no-dependency death cases.	When fund exceeds $2,000,000, excise may be reduced to 4% and suspended when fund exceeds $2,500,000.
ILLINOIS	Second injury involving loss or loss of use of major members or eye which added to pre-existing loss of member results in permanent total disability.	Disability caused by second injury.*	Difference between compensation payable for second injury and permanent total disability.	Semi-yearly employer payment of .125% of compensation payments.	When fund reaches $500,000 amount payable into fund reduced by 1/2. When fund reaches $600,000, payments cease. When fund reduced to $400,000, payment of 1/2 amount required. When fund is reduced to $300,000, payment of full amount shall be resumed.
INDIANA	Second injury involving loss or loss of use of hand, arm, foot, leg, or eye which added to pre-existing loss or loss of use of member results in permanent total disability.	Disability caused by second injury.	Difference between compensation payable for second injury and permanent total disability.	1% of compensation paid by insurers and self-insurers during preceding calendar year.	Payment suspended when fund reaches $400,000.

Calif. *Second injury must account for 35% unless prior disability involved a major member and second injury was to opposite and corresponding member and accounts for at least 5%. No benefits payable for subsequent unrelated noncompensable injury.

Conn. *Fund also pays accident and health insurance coverage for injured employees when employer moves out of state or goes out of business.

Ill. *Employer is liable in full if second injury is permanent and total without relation to prior injury.

CHART XIII ☐ SECOND-INJURY FUNDS ☐ January 1, 1989 (continued)

JURISDICTION	INJURIES COVERED	PAYABLE BY EMPLOYER	PAYABLE BY FUND	SOURCE OF FUND	SPECIAL PROVISIONS
IOWA	Second injury involving loss or loss of use of member or eye which added to pre-existing loss of use of member results in permanent disability.	Disability caused by second injury.	Difference between compensation payable for second injury and permanent disability, less value of previous loss of member or organ.	$2,000 in dependent death cases; $5,000 in no-dependent death cases; any contributions by the United States; payments due but not paid to non-resident alien dependents; and sums recovered from third parties.	Payments suspended when fund reaches $500,000, resumed when below $300,000.
KANSAS	Second injury related to 17 types of handicap as listed in statute—any physical or mental impairment.	Difference between fund payment and maximum award.	Compensation to the extent pre-existing handicap contributed to second injury.	$18,500 from employer in no-dependency death cases, and pro-rata annual assessment upon carriers and self-insurers based on losses.	Legislature oversees adequacy of workers' compensation fund, administered by Insurance Commissioner. Employer must prove knowledge of prior disability.*
KENTUCKY	Second injury or disease which added to prior disability or condition results in permanent disability greater than from second injury alone.	Disability caused by second injury or dormant condition.	Difference between compensation payable for second injury and greater disability, less amount paid for prior injury.	3/4% premium tax on carriers and self-insurers for administration and variable assessment based on need.	
LOUISIANA	Second injury which combined with prior permanent partial disability results in disability greater than from second injury alone, or in death.*	Total disability benefits for first 104 weeks; in death cases, first 175 weeks; 50% of medical benefits which exceed $5,000 but are less than $10,000, and 100% thereafter.	Employer reimbursed for balance of benefits.	2.0% premium tax on carriers and self-insurers, minimum $10.	Assessments reduced at discretion of the Board with 30 days written notice before assessment is due.
MAINE	Second injury caused by accident, disease, or congenital condition, which added to pre-existing impairment results in permanent total disability.	Disability caused by second injury.	Fund reimburses employer for compensation payments not attributable to the second injury.	In no-dependency death cases, 100 x SAWW and civil penalties of up to $10,000 assesed against employers who fail to insure.	Duplicate payments from Second Injury Fund and Employment Rehabilitation Fund prohibited.
MARYLAND	Second injury which combined with a pre-existing permanent impairment due to accident, disease, or cogenital condition results in a greater combined disability constituting a hindrance to employment.	Disability caused by second injury.	If permanent disability exceeds 50% of the body as a whole, employee is entitled to additional compensation for the full disability from the "Subsequent Injury Fund." Prior injury and second injury must each be compensable for at least 125 weeks.	6.5% of compensation on all awards and settlement agreements.	
MASSACHUSETTS	Second injury which added to pre-existing physical impairment results in substantially greater disability or death. Pre-existing disability must support 25% earnings loss or 90 weeks of benefits.	Benefits for first 104 weeks.	Employer reimbursed for 75% of benefits after first 104 weeks.	$500 in no-dependency death cases, and additional $500 in every death case; unpaid balance of scheduled awards.	Pro-rata assessment based on losses paid during preceding year by carriers and self-insureds.
MICHIGAN	Second injury involving loss of member or eye, which added to pre-existing loss of member results in permanent total disability.	Disability caused by second injury.	Difference between compensation payable for second injury and permanent total disability. Benefits for employee with more than one job but for whom injury occurred on job which represented less than 80% AWW. For workers certified "vocationally handicapped," fund pays benefits after 52 weeks.	Assessments on carriers and self-insurers proportionate to 175% of disbursements from fund to annual compensation benefits paid.	Fund is credited with any balance in excess of $200,000.*

MINNESOTA	Second injury that results in substantially greater disability than would have resulted from second injury alone.	Disability caused by second injury.	Employer reimbursed for disability after 52 weeks, medical after $2,000. If second injury results in permanent partial disability, fund pays wage replacement benefits beyond deductible.	$25,000 in no-dependency death cases, 31% of compensation for current indemnity payments, which finances all fund obligations; assessment based on various factors for injuries occuring after 1/1/84; certain penalties.	Commissioner determines assessment base and rate dependent on fund's financial position and increasing up to 12% annually.
	Second injury that would not have occurred except for the pre-existing physical impairment.	All compensation due.	Employer reimbursed for all compensation.		
MISSISSIPPI	Second injury involving loss or loss of use of member or eye, which added to pre-existing loss or loss of use of member or eye results in permanent total disability.	Disability caused by second injury.	Difference between compensation payable for second injury and permanent disability.	$500 in no-dependency death cases; $300 in dependency cases. Commission may transfer up to $200,000 from Administrative Expense Fund.	Payments suspended when fund reaches $350,000 and resumed when fund reduced to $150,000.
MISSOURI	Second injury resulting in permanent partial disability which compounds either a greater permanent partial or a permanent total disability.	Disability caused by second injury.	Difference between compensation payable for second injury and compounded disability.	Surcharge on all workers' compensation premiums not to exceed 3% of premiums, paid by all insureds and self-insurers.	Surcharge suspended when fund reaches $24,000,000 and resumed when fund is reduced to $12,000,000.
MONTANA	Second injury which combined with prior permanent physical impairment results in death or disability.	Insurer liable for payment of benefits for first 104 weeks.	Employer reimbursed after first 104 weeks.	$1000 paid by employers, insurers, or accident fund in every death case. Carriers and self-insurers assessed 5% of losses paid in preceding year.	Division must certify worker as vocationally handicapped.
NEBRASKA	Second injury which combined with pre-existing disability causes substantially greater disability. Pre-existing disability must support 25% earnings loss or 90 weeks of benefits.[1]	Disability caused by second injury.	Difference between compensation payable for second injury and the total resulting disability.	1% premium tax on carriers or self-insurers ($25 minimum) payable to Workers' Compensation Court.	Payments suspended when fund reaches $400,000. Assessment (1%) when fund reduced to $200,000.
NEVADA	Second injury which combined with any previous permanent physical disability causes substantially greater disability.*		Compensation allocated between insurer and fund.	Subsequent Injury Fund in state treasury.**	Compensable claim considered "excess loss" in calculation of employer's experience rating. Employer must prove knowledge of prior impairment.
NEW HAMPSHIRE	Second injury which combined with any pre-existing disability results in substantially greater disability.[1]	Benefits for first 104 weeks.	Employer reimbursed after first 104 weeks.	Assessment against carriers and self-insurers proportional to total benefits paid by all carriers.	
NEW JERSEY	Second injury resulting in permanent partial disability which added to pre-existing partial disability, compensable or not, results in permanent total disability.	Disability caused by compensable injury.	Difference between compensation payable for second injury and permanent total disability.	Annual surcharge on policyholders and self-insured employers of pro-rata percentage of 150% of payments estimated to be paid from fund during forthcoming year. Annual surcharge paid quarterly.	When fund balance exceeds $1,250,000, up to $50,000 per year may be applied toward administration costs of Division.

[1]In death cases it must be established that either the injury or the death would not have occurred except for such pre-existing permanent physical impairment. "Permanent physical impairment" means any permanent condition due to previous accident, disease, or congenital condition which is likely to be a hindrance to employment.

Kan. *Employer may file description of prior impairment to create presumption of prior knowledge.

La. *"Permanent partial disability" means any permanent condition due to injury, disease, or congenital causes which is likely to be a hindrance to employment. Certain scheduled conditions are presumed to be permanent partial disability if employer had prior knowledge.

Mich. *Compensation to certified vocationally handicapped persons payable from fund after 52 weeks.

Minn. *If injury, disability or death would not have occurred but for the preexisting impairment, the fund pays all benefits (except for a cardiac condition, impairment of at least 10% of the whole man, or as prescribed by rule).

Nev. *Pre-existing disability must support a rating of 12% or more of the whole man based on A.M.A. guides, which is likely to be a hindrance to employment.
**Fund is composed of assessments, penalties, bonds, securities, and all other property collected by administrator, Division of Industrial Insurance Regulation.

CHART XIII ☐ SECOND-INJURY FUNDS ☐ January 1, 1989 (continued)

JURISDICTION	INJURIES COVERED	PAYABLE BY EMPLOYER	PAYABLE BY FUND	SOURCE OF FUND	SPECIAL PROVISIONS
NEW MEXICO	Second injury which added to pre-existing disability results in permanent disability greater than from second injury alone; or, second injury resulting in death.	Liability apportioned by Workers' Compensation Administration determination.	Liability apportioned by Workers' Compensation Administration determination.	$1,000 in no-dependency death cases. Employer or insurer pays quarterly assessment up to 3% of compensation paid during quarter, exclusive of attorney's fees.	Employers and insurers have 2 year statute of limitations, from date of notice or knowledge of claim, for claims against the fund.
NEW YORK	Second injury involving loss or loss of use of member or eye, which added to pre-existing injury results in permanent total disability; second injury which added to pre-existing loss or partial loss of member or eye or other "permanent physical impairment" results in disability greater than from second injury alone or second injury or disease resulting in death, which is caused by pre-existing disability.[1]	Benefits for first 104 weeks.	Employer reimbursed after first 104 weeks. Fund also pays any additional benefits due to an employee who was working in concurrent employments when injured.	Assessment against carriers and self-insurers proportional to compensation payments made by all carriers.	Employer or insurer pays awards and medical expenses, but is reimbursed from special disability fund for benefits after first 104 weeks.
NORTH CAROLINA	Second injury involving loss of member or eye which added to pre-existing injury results in permanent total disability, provided the original and increased disability were each 20% of the entire member.*	Disability caused by second injury.	Difference between compensation payable for second injury and permanent total disability.	Assessments against employer or insurer for each permanent partial disability, up to $50 for a minor member and $200 for a major member (currently $25 and $100, respectively).	
NORTH DAKOTA	Second injury or aggravation of any previous injury or condition which results in further disability.	Disability caused by second injury.	Percent attributable to aggravation or second injury.	Benefit Fund.	Compensation in excess of amount chargeable to second injury is charged to general fund.
OHIO	Second injury which aggravates pre-existing disease or condition (25 types of handicaps as listed by statute), resulting in death, temporary or permanent total disability, and disability compensable under a special schedule.*	Disability attributable to injury or occupational disease sustained in employment.	Amount of disability or proportion of cost of death award determined by Industrial Commission to be attributable to employee's pre-existing disability.	Reserve set aside out of statutory surplus funds.	In the case of a self-insuring employer, excess payments are made from the surplus fund. By rule of Commission in the case of State Fund employer, compensation in excess of amount chargeable to second injury is charged to surplus fund.
OKLAHOMA	Second injury to "physically impaired person"* which causes injury to the body as a whole, or to a major member combined with disability to body as a whole. Must exceed 17% to body as a whole.	Disability caused by latest injury.	Difference between compensation payable for prior injuries and compensation for combined injuries.	3% of permanent disability losses by carriers, state fund, and self-insurers, and 3% of awards for permanent disability by injured worker.	Permanent total awards are payable by the fund for five years or until age 65, whichever is longer.
OREGON	Injury caused by preexisting condition (may be congenital) or which combined with preexisting condition results in greater permanent disability.	First $1,000 claims cost and portion of claim for which relief not granted are charged to employer loss experience.	Claims cost above $1,000 and percentage of balance for which Department grants relief.	Employer and worker each pay $.14 per day, for a total of $.28 per worker per day, apportioned to the Workers Reemployment Reserve (Second Injury Fund), Handicapped Workers Reserve, Reopened Claims Reserve and the Retroactive Reserve.	Reimbursement from fund subject to funds available. Percentage of relief granted not reviewable. Settlement of claim requires Department approval if involves reimbursement.

	All injuries occurring during the first 2 years after a preferred worker is hired.	Not applicable.	Premium reimbursed for worker for first two years of employment.	Same as above.	Insurers may not increase employers premium as a result of additional injuries of the workers during the 2 year agreement.
PENNSYLVANIA	Second injury involving loss or loss of use which added to pre-existing loss or loss of use of member results in permanent total disability.	Scheduled benefits as a result of second injury.	Remaining compensation due for total disability.	Assessment against carriers and self-insurers proportional to compensation payments.	Payments are made directly by the Department.
PUERTO RICO	Second injury which aggravates or augments any former disability.		Job injury not caused by work accident is compensated in addition to second injury. Compensation for prior job injury is deducted from compensation payable for total disability, except where combined injury results in permanent total disability, which is compensated as such.	Insurance premiums.	The difference between expenditures by the Industrial Commission and the Manager of the State Insurance Fund and their maximum budget allotment are placed in the Reserve Fund for catastrophes except for medical expense surpluses; maximum $1 million.
RHODE ISLAND	Second injury which merges with pre-existing work-related disability resulting in greater disability or death.	Benefits for first 52 weeks.*	Employer reimbursed after first 52 weeks.*	2-3/4% tax on gross premiums collected from insurers and comparable tax on self-insurers, plus $750 in no-dependency death cases; also certain penalties.	Employer must prove knowledge of prior injury unless employee failed to disclose. Tax may be reduced when fund reaches $2 million.
SOUTH CAROLINA	Second injury which added to any previous permanent physical impairment results in substantially greater disability or death.	Disability caused by second injury for first 78 weeks' compensation and medical care.	Employer reimbursed for all benefits after 78 weeks, plus 50% of medical payments over $3000 during first 78 weeks.	Pro-rata assessments on carriers and self-insurers based on losses paid. In no-dependency deaths, unpaid benefits to fund.	Employer must prove prior knowledge of impairment or that worker was unaware of impairment.*
SOUTH DAKOTA	Second injury which combined with any pre-existing disability, results in additional permanent partial or total disability or death.	Disability caused by second injury.	Difference between compensation payable for second injury and compensation for combined injuries.	Carriers and self-insurers assessed 1% of losses paid during preceding year and $500 in no-dependency death cases.	Payments suspended at $200,000, and resumed at $100,000.
TENNESSEE	Second injury involving loss or loss of use of member or eye, which added to pre-existing loss or loss of use of member results in permanent total disability.*	Disability caused by second injury.	Benefits in excess of 100% total disability to body as a whole.	50% of revenues from the 4% premium tax on insurers and self-insurers.	
TEXAS	Second injury which added to pre-existing injury results in permanent total disability.	Disability caused by second injury.	Difference between compensation payable for second injury and permanent total disability.	Maximum $85,680* payable into fund in each no-dependency death case.	The Industrial Accident Board has right of subrogation to recover claims and attorney's fees paid from Second Injury Funds.
UTAH	Second injury which combined with a previous permanent incapacity due to accident, disease, or congenital condition results in permanent total disability.	First $20,000 of medical benefits and first 3 years of permanent total disability compensation.	50% of medical expenses in excess of $20,000 and permanent total disability compensation after initial 3 year period.	Up to 7.15% premium tax on insurers and self-insurers. Fines from uninsured employers.	If employee is permanently and totally disabled, employer or insurance carrier credited for all prior payments of temporary total, temporary partial and permanent partial disability compensation.

N.C. *Epilepsy is considered a prior permanent disability.

Ohio *Does not apply to compensation for temporary partial or percentage of permanent partial disability.

Okla. *"Physically impaired person" is one who, by accident, disease, birth, military action, or any other cause, has suffered the loss of sight of one eye, the loss by amputation of the whole or a part of, or loss of use of, a major member of his body.

R.I. *For claims filed after 5/18/85. Employer reimbursed after first 104 weeks for claims filed before 5/18/85.

S.C. *"Permanent physical impairment" means any permanent condition due to injury, disease, or congenital causes which is likely to be a hindrance to employment. Certain scheduled conditions are presumed to be permanent physical impairment if employer had prior knowledge.

Tenn. *Also covers death or disablement resulting from injuries of an epileptic seizure occurring on or after 7/1/85.

Texas *360 times maximum weekly benefit.

CHART XIII ☐ SECOND-INJURY FUNDS ☐ January 1, 1989 (continued)

JURISDICTION	INJURIES COVERED	PAYABLE BY EMPLOYER	PAYABLE BY FUND	SOURCE OF FUND	SPECIAL PROVISIONS
VERMONT	Second injury involving loss of use of member or eye which added to previous disability results in permanent total disability	Disability caused by second injury.	Difference between compensation payable for second injury and permanent total disability.	$500 in no-dependency death cases.	
VIRGIN ISLANDS	Second injury which combined with prior impairment results in death or compensable disability greater than from second injury alone	None. Employer's experience rating affected by disability payments after 104 weeks.	All benefits	Premiums paid by employers by classification and experience, plus fines, penalties, and interest.	Employer must have prior knowledge of disability.
VIRGINIA	Second injury involving 20% loss or loss of use of member or eye which added to pre-existing disability of 20% or more results in total or partial disability.	Disability caused by second injury.	Employer reimbursed for compensation after all other compensation has expired plus up to $7,500 each for medical and vocational rehabilitation expenses.	1/4% premium tax on carriers and self-insurers.	Payments suspended at $250,000, and resumed at $125,000.
WASHINGTON	Second injury or disease which added to pre-existing injury or disease results in permanent total disability or death.	Disability caused by second injury.	Difference between charge assessed against employer at time of second injury and total pension reserve.	Transfer of not more than cost from accident fund to second injury account. Self-insurers pay proportional to claims against self-insurers.	Preferred workers* have all benefits for claims arising within 3 years of new employment paid Second Injury Fund.
WEST VIRGINIA	Second injury which combined with a definitely ascertainable physical impairment caused by a permanent injury results in permanent total disability	Disability caused by second injury.	Remainder of the compensation that would be due for permanent total disability.	Self insureds pay 15% of manual rates; remainder allocated to funding from premiums paid by regular subscribers.	Self-insured employer who has not elected to pay into the fund liable for full compensation of permanent total disability from combined effect of a previous injury and a second injury.
WISCONSIN	Second injury with permanent disability for 200 weeks or more with a pre-existing disability of an equal degree or greater.	Disability caused by second injury.	Disability caused by lesser of 2 injuries. If the combined disabilities result in permanent total disability, fund pays the difference between compensation payable for second injury and permanent total disability.	$5,000 in death cases, $7,000 for loss of a hand, arm, foot, leg, or eye 100% of death benefit in no-dependency death cases.	
WYOMING	Second injury in extra-hazardous employment which added to pre-existing loss or loss of use of member or eye results in permanent total disability.	Disability caused by second injury.	Difference between compensation payable for second injury and permanent disability.	$500 in no-dependency death cases.	Any payments for previous partial disability or payments which would have been made if the previous injury had occurred in an extra-hazardous employment are deducted from the award.
LONGSHORE ACT	Second injury resulting in permanent partial disability which added to pre-existing injury results in permament total disability.	Disability caused by second injury for first 104 weeks.	Difference between compensation payable for second injury and permament total disability.	$5,000 in no-dependency death cases or unpaid awards. Pro-rata assessments based on losses paid. Fines and penalties.	50% of fund is for second injuries and 50% for rehabilitation. Supplementary benefits for total disability or death payable by fund.

Wash. *Defined as workers who must change jobs due to effect of an industrial injury or illness.

APPENDIX H
Workers' Compensation Administrative Offices

WORKERS' COMPENSATION ADMINISTRATIVE OFFICES

U.S. DEPARTMENT OF LABOR

Employment Standards Administration
200 Constitution Ave., N.W.
Washington, D.C. 20210
202-523-6191

Workers' Compensation Programs
Office of State Liaison and Legislative Analysis
200 Constitution Ave., N.W. Rm. N-4414
Washington, D.C. 20210
202-523-9575

STATE OFFICES

ALABAMA
Department of Industrial Relations
Workmen's Compensation Office
Montgomery, Alabama 36130
205-261-2868

ALASKA
Workers' Compensation Division
Department of Labor
P.O. Box 1149
Juneau, Alaska 99802
907-465-2790

ARIZONA
Industrial Commission
800 W. Washington Street
P.O. Box 19070
Phoenix, Arizona 85007
602-255-4661

ARKANSAS
Workers' Compensation Commission
Justice Building
State Capitol Grounds
Little Rock, Arkansas 72201
501-372-3930

CALIFORNIA
Division of Industrial Accidents
P.O. Box 603, Room 103
San Francisco, California 94101
415-557-3542

COLORADO
Division of Labor
1313 Sherman Street, Room 314
Denver, Colorado 80203
303-866-2861

CONNECTICUT
Workers' Compensation Commission
1890 Dixwell Ave.
Hamden, Connecticut 06514
203-789-7783

DELAWARE
Industrial Accident Board
State Office Building, 6th Floor
820 North French Street
Wilmington, Delaware 19801
302-571-2884

DISTRICT OF COLUMBIA
D.C. Department of Employment Services
1200 Upshur Street, N.W.
Washington, D.C. 20011
202-576-6265

FLORIDA
Division of Workers' Compensation
1321 Executive Center Drive East
Tallahassee, Florida 32399-0680
904-488-2548

GEORGIA
Board of Workers' Compensation
South Tower, Suite 1000
One CNN Center
Atlanta, Georgia 30303
404-656-3875

HAWAII
Disability Compensation Division
Department of Labor and Industrial Relations
830 Punchbowl Street
Honolulu, Hawaii 96813
808-548-4131

IDAHO
Industrial Commission
317 Main Street
Boise, Idaho 83720
208-334-6000

ILLINOIS
Industrial Commission
100 W. Randolph St., Suite 8-200
Chicago, Illinois 60601
312-917-6555

INDIANA
Industrial Board
601 State Office Building
100 N. Senate Avenue
Indianapolis, Indiana 46204
317-232-3808

IOWA
Industrial Commission
507 10th Street
Des Moines, Iowa 50319
515-281-5934

KANSAS
Division of Workers' Compensation
900 S.W. Jackson, Room 651-5
Topeka, Kansas 66612-1276
913-296-3441

KENTUCKY
Workers' Compensation Board
U.S. 127 South, 127 Building
Frankfort, Kentucky 40601
502-564-5550

LOUISIANA
Office of Workers' Compensation
P.O. Box 94094
910 N. Bon Marche Drive
Baton Rouge, Louisiana 70806-2288
504-925-7211

MAINE
Workers' Compensation Commission
Station 27, Deering Building
Augusta, Maine 04333
207-289-3751

MARYLAND
Workmen's Compensation Commission
6 N. Liberty St.
Baltimore, Maryland 21201
301-659-4700

MASSACHUSETTS
Department of Industrial Accidents
600 Washington Street
7th Floor
Boston, Massachusetts 02111
617-727-4300

MICHIGAN
Workers' Disability Compensation Office
Department of Labor
P.O. Box 30016
Lansing, Michigan 48909
517-373-3480

MINNESOTA
Department of Labor and Industry
444 Lafayette Road
St. Paul, Minnesota 55101
612-296-2432

MISSISSIPPI
Workers' Compensation Commission
P.O. Box 5300
Jackson, Mississippi 39216
601-987-4200

MISSOURI
Division of Workers' Compensation
Department of Labor & Industrial Relations
P.O. Box 58, 722 Jefferson St.
Jefferson City, Missouri 65102
314-751-4231

MONTANA
Division of Workers' Compensation
P.O. Box 537
5 S. Last Chance Gulch
Helena, Montana 59601
406-444-6500

NEBRASKA
Workmen's Compensation Court
State House
Lincoln, Nebraska 68509
402-471-2568

NEVADA
State Industrial Insurance System
515 E. Musser Street
Carson City, Nevada 89714
702-885-5284

NEW HAMPSHIRE
Department of Labor
19 Pillsbury Street
Concord, New Hampshire 03301
603-271-3171

NEW JERSEY
Division of Workers' Compensation
Department of Labor
Call No. 381
John Fitch Plaza, CN 110
Trenton, New Jersey 08625
609-292-2414

NEW MEXICO
Workers' Compensation Division
Department of Labor
700 4th St., S.W.
P.O. Box 27198
Santa Fe, New Mexico 87502
505-841-8787

NEW YORK
Workers' Compensation Board
180 Livingston Street
Brooklyn, N.Y. 11248
718-802-6600

NORTH CAROLINA
Industrial Commission
Dobbs Building
430 N. Salisbury Street
Raleigh, N. Carolina 27611
919-733-4820

NORTH DAKOTA
Workmens' Compensation Bureau
Russell Building—Highway 83 N.
4007 N. State Street
Bismarck, N. Dakota 58501
701-224-2700

OHIO
Bureau of Workers' Compensation
246 N. High Street
Columbus, Ohio 43266-0581
614-466-2950

OKLAHOMA
1915 North Stiles
2101 N. Lincoln
Oklahoma City, Oklahoma 73105
405-557-7600

OREGON
Workers' Compensation Department
Labor and Industries Building
Salem, Oregon 97310
503-378-4100

PENNSYLVANIA
Bureau of Workers' Compensation
Labor and Industry Building
3607 Derry Street
Harrisburg, Pennsylvania 17111
717-783-5421

PUERTO RICO
Industrial Commission of Puerto Rico
G.P.O. Box 4466
San Juan, Puerto Rico 00936
809-783-2028

RHODE ISLAND
Division of Workers' Compensation
610 Manton Avenue
P.O. Box 3500
Providence, Rhode Island 02909
401-272-0700

SOUTH CAROLINA
Worker's Compensation Fund
1612 Marion Street
P.O. Box 1715
Columbia, South Carolina 29202
803-737-5700

SOUTH DAKOTA
Department of Labor
Division on Labor and Management
700 N. Illinois Street
Pierre, South Dakota 57501
605-773-3681

TENNESSEE
Division of Workers' Compensation
Department of Labor
501 Union Building, 2nd Floor
Nashville, Tennessee 37219
615-741-2395

TEXAS
Industrial Accident Board
200 East Riverside Drive
Austin, Texas 78704
512-448-7900

UTAH
Industrial Commission
160 East 300 South
Salt Lake City, Utah 84145-0580
801-530-6800

VERMONT
Department of Labor and Industry
State Office Building
120 State St.
Montpelier, Vermont 05602
802-828-2286

VIRGINIA
Industrial Commission
P.O. Box 1794
1000 DMV Building
Richmond, Virginia 23214
804-257-8600

WASHINGTON
Department of Labor and Industries
General Administration Building, HC-101
Olympia, Washington 98504
206-753-6307

WEST VIRGINIA
Workers' Compensation Fund
Department of Labor
601 Morris Square
Box 3151
Charleston, West Virginia 25332
304-348-2580

WISCONSIN
Workers' Compensation Division
P.O. Box 7901
Madison, Wisconsin 53707
608-266-1340

WYOMING
Workers' Compensation Division
122 West 25th St., 2nd Floor,
Cheyenne, Wyoming 82002-0700
307-777-7441

NOTES

CHAPTER 1 OVERVIEW

The Longshore and Harborworkers' Compensation Act is found at 33 U.S.C. §§901 *et seq.*; the Federal Employees' Compensation Act is found at 5 U.S.C. §§8101 *et seq.*

TYPES OF CLAIMS

In *U.S. Industries/Federal Sheet Metal, Inc. v. Director, Office of Workers' Comp. Programs* (1982), the U.S. Supreme Court held that a "claim" under the Longshore and Harborworkers' Compensation Act must contain "a statement of the time, place, nature and cause of injury." Compare this requirement to the D.C. Court of Appeals rule that, under D.C. law, "a claim means nothing more than a simple request for compensation which triggers the process of claim adjudication." *Fierreira v. D.C. Dept. of Employment Services* (1987).

Distinctions Between Injuries and Occupational Diseases

The Wyoming law referred to is Wyo. Stat. §27-12-102(xii)(A). Other state and federal statutes referred to in the section are:

Alaska Stat. §23-30.265(13); Cal. Labor Code §3208 (§3208.1 provides that an injury may be "specific" or "cumulative," while §§4401, *et seq.* make explicit provision for asbestosis); Hawaii Rev. Stat. §386-3; Mass. Gen. Laws Ann. ch. 152, §§1.7(A) and 26; Wis. Stat. §§102.01(1)-(2)(g), 102.03(1)(a), (e); 33 U.S.C. §913(a), (b)(2) (Longshore and Harborworkers' Compensation Act, §§13(a) and 13(b)(2) provide time limitations for occupational diseases); 5 U.S.C. §8101(5) (Federal Employees' Compensation Act).

For a discussion of the effectiveness of the different approaches taken by Michigan and Ohio with regard to safety code violations, *see* Sands, *How Effective is Safety Legislation?* 11 J.L. ECON. 165 (1968).

EMPLOYMENTS COVERED

Statutes referred to in this section are S.C. Code Ann. §§42-1-130, -150, -320, -350, -360, -370, -400, -410, -420, -480, -490, and 42-7-60 (South Carolina's Workers' Compensation Law); Texas Rev. Civ. Stat. Ann. art. 8306, §§2, 3a, 19, and art. 8309, §§1, 1a; and Wyo. Stat. §§27-12-102, -106, -108 (Wyoming Workers' Compensation Law).

CHAPTER 2 INJURIES AND ACCIDENTS

The Montana description of a compensable injury is found at Mont. Code Ann. §39-17-119.

IN THE COURSE OF AND ARISING OUT OF EMPLOYMENT

In the Course of Employment

Employees at an employment-sponsored function: Nev. Rev. Stat. §§616.110, -.270 exclude injuries sustained at social gathering unless the workers are paid; Cal. Labor Code §§3208, 3600 states that voluntary participation in off-duty sports events are not covered; Ohio Rev. Code §4123.01(c)(3) permits an employee to waive coverage at recreational or fitness activity.

Going and Coming

The New Jersey Supreme Court presented a good discussion of the general rule that injuries sustained while traveling between home and a fixed situs of employment are not compensable and applications of the rule in *Hammond v. Great Atlantic & Pacific Tea Co.*, 56 N.J. 7, 264 A.2d 204 (1970).

Injuries Caused by the Worker's Own Fault

Negligence; Purposeful Self-Infliction. Wyo. Stat. §27-12-102 precludes compensation for injuries "caused totally" by employees' negligence.

No listing of sources is given here for exclusion of injuries "intentionally" caused—even though not all workers' compensation laws have such exceptions—since, by definition, such injuries do not arise out of employment.

Willful Misconduct. The term "willful misconduct" or its equivalent (indicated in parentheses) appears in Ala. Code §25-5-51 ("wilful violation of law"); Conn. Gen. Stat. §31-284; N.H. Rev. Stat. §§281:2, :15; S.D. Codified Laws 62-4-37; Va.-W.C. Act Sec. 65.1-23.1; Federal Employees' Compensation Act.

Nebraska's Act, Neb. Rev. Stat. §§48-101, -127 uses the oxymoronic term, "intentional negligence"; 77 Pa. Stat. Ann. §201 precludes compensation for injuries caused by "reckless indifference to danger"; P. R. Laws Ann. tit.11, §§2, 5, denies compensation "when recklessness on the part of the employee is the sole cause of injury."

Safety Violations as Separate Employer Defense. Statutory provisions: Fla. Stat. §§29-440.09(4) provides for a 25 percent reduction in compensation for injuries caused by willful refusal to use safety devices or to observe a required safety rule, while Mo. Rev. Stat. §287-120-5 provides for reduction in compensation by 15 percent if the injury was caused by employee's intentional and knowing failure to obey posted safety rules or to use safety devices and if employer had made an effort to cause employees to use such devices; Ala. Code §25-5-51 provides for nonrecovery for injuries caused by neglecting to use a safety device provided by employer; Del. Code Ann. tit. 19, §§2301, 2353 (failure to use safety devices); Ga. Code §§34-9-1, 34-9-17 excludes compensation for injuries caused by "misconduct or failure to comply with safety rules"; Ind. Code §22-3-2-8 ("neglect in using a safety appliance, failure or refusal to obey a written or printed rule of the employer"); Okla. Stat. tit. 85, §§3, 4, 11, provides that benefits are not payable for injuries resulting from intentional failure to use required safety devices; similarly, Kan. Stat. Ann. §§44-501, -503; La. Rev. Stat. Ann. §§23.1021, -.1081; Tenn. Code Ann. §§50-902, -910; Va. Code §65.1-23.1.

Intoxication. For a discussion of the general rule, *see* Larson, *Intoxication as a Defense in Workmen's Compensation*, 59 CORN. L. REV. 398 (1974).

Workers' compensation statutes that preclude recovery for injuries caused by the employee's own intoxication are Ala. Code §25-5-51; Alaska Stat. §§23.30.055, -.30.80 (injuries caused "solely" by intoxication); Ark. Stat. Ann. §81-1305; Cal. Labor Code §§3208, 3600; Conn. Gen. Stat. §31-284; Del. Code Ann. tit. 19, §§2301, 2353; D.C. Code Ann. §36-303(d) (no liability if injury is caused "solely" by employee's intoxication); Fla. Stat. §29-440.09(3) (no compensation for injuries caused "primarily" by intoxication); Hawaii Rev. Stat. §386-3; Idaho Code §§72-102, 72-208; Ind. Code § 22-3-2-8; Iowa Code §§85.16, 85.64; Kan. Stat. Ann. §§44-501, 44-503; Ky. Rev. Stat. §§342.610,

342.620; La. Rev. Stat. Ann. §§23.1021, 23.1081; Md. Ann. Code art. 101, §15; Minn. Stat. §§176.011, -.012; Miss. Code Ann. §71-3-7; Neb. Rev. Stat. §§48-101, -127; Nev. Rev. Stat. §§616.110, -.270; N.H. Rev. Stat. Ann. §§281:2, -:15; N.J. Rev. Stat. §34:15-7; N.M. Stat. Ann. §§52-1-10, -11, -12; N.Y. Work. Comp. Law §§67-10, -15, -201; N.C. Gen. Stat. §§97-2, -12; N.D. Cent. Code §§65-05-28; Okla. Stat. tit. 85 §§3, 4, 11; 77 Pa. Stat. Ann. §201; P.R. Laws Ann. tit. 11 §§2, 5 ("provided intoxication caused the accident"); R.I. Gen. Laws §28-33-2; S.C. Code Ann. §§42-1-160, -9-60; S.D. Codified Laws §62-4-37; Tenn. Code Ann. §§50-902, -910; Tex. Rev. Civ. Stat. Ann. art. 8309-1; Vt. Stat. Ann. tit. §§618, 649; Va. Code §65.1-23.1; W. Va. §23-4-2; Wyo. Stat. §27-12-102.

Ga. Code §§34-9-1, 34-9-17 states that alcoholism will not be considered an injury arising out of employment; Me. Rev. Stat. Ann. tit. 39, §51 states that the intoxication exception does not apply if the employer knew the employee was intoxicated while on duty or that employee was in habit of becoming intoxicated.

MENTAL STRESS CLAIMS

For a useful survey and analysis of this topic, *see* BNA Special Report, *Stress in the Workplace: Costs, Liabilities, and Prevention* (1987).

CHAPTER 3 OCCUPATIONAL DISEASES

The source for the quote is A. LARSON, WORKMEN'S COMPENSATION LAW, Section 41.32 (1986). See also LARSON, section 41.31.

OCCUPATIONAL DISEASE COVERAGE

Scheduled Diseases

The quote is again from Larson, in *Occupational Disease Under Workmen's Compensation Law*, 9 U. RICH. L. REV. 87, 89 (1974).

N.Y. Work. Comp. Law §3; Ohio Rev. Code Ann. §§4123.68; N.C. Gen. Stat. §97-53.

Other Diseases

Hearing loss: N.Y. Work. Comp. Law §§49aa–49ee; Wis. Stat. 102.555; Ohio Rev. Code Ann. §4123.57.

Mental disabilities or stress-caused illnesses: The trend toward allowance of mental-distress claims, whether as injury or as an occupational disease has been noted in 21 LA. L. REV. 868 (1961) and 109 PA. L. REV. 1185 (1961).

PRE-EXISTING CONDITIONS

Ill. Rev. Stat. ch.48, §172.36(d).

APPORTIONMENT AND ALLOCATION OF COSTS OF OCCUPATIONAL DISEASE CLAIMS

Apportionment: Kan. Stat. Ann. §44-5a01(d).

Allocation of costs to employer of last injurious exposure: Ala. Code §25-5-147 (special rule regarding pneumoconiosis and radiation, §§25-5-146, -196); Colo. Rev. Stat. §8-51-112; D.C. Code Ann. §36-310; Fla. Stat. §440.151(5); Idaho Code §72-102(17)(c); Ind. Stats. [Ann.] §22-3-7-33; Iowa Code §85A.10; 77 Pa. Stat. Ann. §1401(g); S.D. Codified Laws §62-8-15; Tenn. Code Ann. §50-6-304; Vt. Stat. Ann. tit. 21, §1008.

SPECIAL CONDITIONS OF COVERAGE (TIME LIMITATIONS)

The quote from Larson appears at LARSON'S WORKMEN'S COMPENSATION LAW, Section 41.82 (1986).

BENEFITS

Ala. Code §25-5-172; Ark. Stat. Ann. §81-1314(b)(3); Idaho Code §72-444; Mont. Code Ann. §39-72-703; Ohio Rev. Code Ann. §4123.68; S.D. Codified Laws §62-8-20; Tenn. Code Ann. §50-6-303(b); 77 Pa. Stat. Ann. §1401(a)(2).

CHAPTER 4 DEATH CLAIMS

WORK-RELATEDNESS OF SUICIDE

For a general discussion, *see* A. Larson, *The Suicide Defense in Workmen's Compensation*, 23 BUFFALO L. REV. 43 (1973).

CHAPTER 5 COMPENSATION AND BENEFITS

THE CONCEPT OF DISABILITY AND DISABILITY COMPENSATION

The restrictive language that the *Allen* court was struggling with appears in 42 U.S.C. §423. Nev. Rev. Stat. §616.605 contains explicit reference to AMA *Guides*.

PERMANENT TOTAL DISABILITY

Utah Code Ann. §§31-5-67, 35-2-15(1).

TEMPORARY PARTIAL DISABILITY

D.C. Code Ann. §36-308(a)(3)(V) provides for wage-loss compensation, while §36-308(c) provides for temporary partial disability compensation, calculated exactly the same way.

Wage Loss

D.C. Code Ann. §36-308(a)(3)(V).

Change of Occupations

Mont. Code Ann. §39-72-405; N.C. Gen. Stat. §97-61.5; Ohio Rev. Code Ann. §4123.47(D), (E); Utah Code Ann. §35-2-56(3), (4).

REHABILITATION

Ohio Rev. Code Ann. §4121.61 and .63 provide for costs of treatment for non-occupational medical conditions.

Jurisdictions in which continued receipt of benefits is conditioned upon entry in or cooperation with rehabilitation authority include Ala. Code §25-5-77(d); Alaska Stat. §23.30.191; Del. Code Ann. §2343, 2353; D.C. Code Ann. §36.307(d); Fla. Stats. Ann. §440.49 (which provides for reduction in benefits by 50 percent for each week of refusal); Kan. Stat. Ann. §44-510g; Ky. Rev. Stat. §342.710 (50 percent reduction in compensation); La. Rev. Stat. §23.1226 (50 percent reduction in compensation); Md. Code Ann. Art. 101 §36; Mont. Code Ann. §39-71-1001-4; N.J. Rev. Stat. §34:15-12 (permanent total disability benefits may stop after 450 weeks unless claimant has submitted to retraining); N.C. Gen. Stat. §97-25; N.D. Cent. Code §65-05.1-04; Or. Rev. Stat. §656.325; R.I. Gen. Laws §28-33-41 (suspension for "willful refusal" of rehabilitation); Vt. Stat. Ann. tit. 21, §641; Va. Code §65.1-88; Wash. Rev. Code §51.36.050 (50 percent reduction in compensation).

Minn. Stat. §176.102 provides for rehabilitation services for dependent surviving spouses for the purpose of making them self-sufficient.

COMPENSATION FOR MEDICAL IMPAIRMENT (PERMANENT PARTIAL DISABILITY)

Nev. Rev. Stat. §616.605; Kansas Stat. Ann. §44-510e; Ky. Rev. Stat. §432.620.

MEDICAL BENEFITS

D.C. Code Ann. §36-307(h) recognizes "spiritual treatment" upon which a claimant relies "in good faith." The pun also appears in Or. Rev. Stat. §656.010. Minn. Stat. §176.135 recognizes Christian Scientist treatment.

CHAPTER 6 JURISDICTION AND PROCEDURE

CONFLICT OF LAWS

Conflicts with Federal Jurisdiction

For discussion of conflicts between local law and admiralty and maritime jurisdiction, *see* Larson, *Conflicts Between Seamen's Remedies and Workmen's Compensation Acts* (1972) 40 FORDHAM L. REV. 473; 1 41WORKMEN'S COMP. L. REV. 369.

Minimal Contacts with Forum State

For discussions of jurisdictional limitations, *see* Larson, *Constitutional Law Conflicts and Workmen's Compensation*, 1971 DUKE L.J. 1037; *Forum Commission Enforcement of Foreign Workmen's Compensation Acts* (1966) 34 U. CHI. L. REV. 177; *and* W. S. MALONE, M. L. PLANT, J. W. LITTLE, WORKERS' COMPENSATION AND EMPLOYMENT RIGHTS, CASES AND MATERIALS (2d ed. 1982), pp. 462, *et seq*.

Statutory Provisions

Ohio Rev. Code Ann. §4123.54, appears to make it impossible for anyone who enters a contract of hire in Ohio to be free of Ohio coverage.

Ala. Code §25-5-35 (1975); Hawaii Rev. Stat. §386-6; Cal. Labor Code §5305; Mich. Comp. Laws §418.845.

JURISDICTION TO MODIFY A FINAL ORDER

Fraud

Burdens of proof in fraud cases, *see* MCCORMICK ON EVIDENCE §340 (2d ed. 1972) *and* 9 WIGMORE ON EVIDENCE, §2498 (1940).

PROCEDURES

Rehearings appear not to be required by the Due Process Clause of the U.S. Constitution. In *NLRB v. Donnelly Garment Co.*, the U.S. Supreme Court found no right to a rehearing in proceedings before the National Labor Relations Board.

CHAPTER 7 ADMINISTRATION

THE AGENCIES

Court-Administered Systems

La. Rev. Stat. Ann., §1311 (West 1950) provides for administration by any district court in the parish in which the injury occurred.

The quoted material is from W. S. MALONE, M. L. PLANT, J. W. LITTLE, WORKERS' COMPENSATION AND EMPLOYMENT RIGHTS, CASES AND MATERIALS, at 400 (2d ed. 1982). Court administration was also criticized in COMPENDIUM OF THE NATIONAL COMMISSION ON STATE WORKMENS' COMPENSATION LAWS at 217 (1973).

See a critical discussion of the New Mexico Decision which may block elimination of court administration of workers' compensation in Note, *Constitutional Law: Administrative Determination of Workmen's Compensation Claims*, 13 OKLA. L. REV. 44 (1960).

Functions of Administrative Agencies

See THE REPORT OF THE NATIONAL COMMISSION ON STATE WORKMEN'S COMPENSATION LAW (1972) at 100 for a listing of the six primary obligations of a workers' compensation program.

Dispute Resolution

See the COMPENDIUM OF THE NATIONAL COMMISSION ON STATE WORKMENS' COMPENSATION LAWS (1973) at 218 and THE REPORT OF THE NATIONAL COMMISSION ON STATE WORKMEN'S COMPENSATION LAW (1972) at 101-102.

CHAPTER 8 JUDICIAL REVIEW

ISSUES REVIEWABLE BY COURT

See THE REPORT OF THE NATIONALCOMMISSION ON STATE WORKMEN'S COMPENSATION LAWS, Recommendation R6.14 (1972).

Minn. Stat. §176.411 requires that agency findings be based on "competent evidence only."

TYPES OF REVIEW AVAILABLE

The statutory authorities for review of workers' compensation by jury trials are: Hawaii Rev. Stats. §§386-73, -78; Md. Code., Art. 101, §§52, 56; Ohio Rev. Code Ann. §4123.519; Vt. Stat. Ann. tit. 21, §§670, 672; Wash. Rev. Code §§51.52.050, -.080, -.104.

CHAPTER 9 EMPLOYER'S PROTECTIONS AND LIABILITIES

IMMUNITY FROM SUIT

Ohio Rev. Code Ann. §§4123.73, -.74 provides for immunity for all injuries arising out of employment.

Changes in Ohio's intentional-tort law are embodied in Ohio Substitute Senate Bill 307, effective August 22, 1986.

GLOSSARY

Accident A sudden, unexpected event that results in or causes a medical harm or injury; physical trauma may also be part of the definition.

Accident (or Injury) claim A claim for workers' compensation benefits filed by a worker who alleges that injury resulted from an accident, to be distinguished in certain jurisdictions from claims for *Occupational disease*.

Aggravation An acceleration, increase in severity, or qualitative worsening of a medical condition brought on by injury, accident, or occupational disease, sometimes considered any permanent worsening of condition, in contradistinction to *Exacerbation*.

Amenable employer Any employer who is subject to workers' compensation law and who is required to obtain workers' compensation coverage or, in those jurisdictions in which coverage is elective, who would be subject to penalties or loss of common-law defenses for failure to obtain coverage.

Arising out of employment One of two prongs of test for work-relatedness of injuries or accidents that asks whether the injury or accident was caused by employment or whether it was caused by forces not connected with employment. See also *In the course of employment*.

Benefits Any award paid under a claim, including compensation payable directly to claimants and payments for health-care providers, rehabilitation services, travel expenses, attorneys' fees, funeral payments, etc. See also *Compensation*.

Burden of proof Degree of proof required to establish a claim or prove a fact. With few exceptions, the burden of proof of each element of a compensable claim is on the claimant and is proof by a preponderance of the evidence. Elements of *Fraud* usually must be proved by clear and convincing evidence, and the burden is on party alleging fraud.

Certified claim A claim that is not disputed by an employer or insurance carrier. See also *Recognized claim*.

Change of occupation Compensation award in certain occupational disease claims in limited number of jurisdictions under which claimants receive fixed amounts for removing themselves from jobs that subjected them to injurious exposure. See also *Occupational disease*.

Claim Any application for workers' compensation benefits filed by an injured or diseased worker or the dependents of a deceased worker. In some places, a claim must include a statement of the time, place, nature, and cause of injury. See also *Accident (or injury) claim; Certified claim; Death claim; Lost-time claim; Medical-only claim; Occupational disease claim; Recognized claim; Safety-code (violation) claim*.

Coming and going rule See *Going and coming rule*.

Compensation Those *benefits* available in workers' compensation systems payable directly to claimants in the form of wage loss, impairment in earnings, impairment in earning capacity, quasi-damages for loss of physical or mental functioning or loss of bodily parts, or, in death claims, survivors' benefits. See also *Permanent partial disability; Permanent total disability; Scheduled-loss award; Temporary partial disability; Temporary total disability*.

(In the) Course of employment One of two prongs of test for work-relatedness of injury or occupational disease that asks whether the time and place of cause of injury or inception of occupational disease bore close enough connection to employment to render it fairly and rationally chargeable to compensation system. See also *Arising out of employment; Going and coming rule; Peculiar to industrial trade or process*.

Death claim A claim for benefits filed usually by surviving dependents of a worker who allegedly was killed in the course of employment; also may be filed in most jurisdictions by non-dependent party who seeks reimbursement for bearing funeral or last-treatment costs of such worker.

Dependent Those individuals defined by statutes as eligible for loss-of-support awards in death claims, usually including spouses, minor children, or other members of deceased worker's family who actually looked to decedent for support before the death or before the injury or occupational disease that caused the death.

Presumed dependents usually include spouses and minor children and, occasionally, parents. Permitted dependents sometimes include other members of decedent's family or household. Individuals not listed in statute as either presumed or permitted dependents generally are ineligible for loss-of-support benefits regardless of whether they were actually dependent upon the decedent for support before the death.

Disability A *Medical impairment* that adversely affects an individual's ability to earn a living or that results in medical treatment. See also *Change of occupations; Permanent partial disability; Permanent total disability; Temporary partial disability; Temporary total disability.*

Exacerbation A worsening of an underlying disease or condition caused by work-related injury, accident, or occupational disease, usually thought of as a passing or one-time "flare-up" of the preexisting problem, in contradistinction to *Aggravation.*

Fraud An intentional falsehood upon which another party relies to his detriment causing damages or change of position. See also *Burden of proof.*

Going and coming rule General rule of noncompensability for those injuries suffered by workers who have a fixed situs of employment while going from home to regular place of employment or coming home from regular place of employment.

Immunity Preclusion of common-law tort actions by employees against co-workers or a complying employer for work-related injuries or diseases.

Impairment See *Medical impairment.*

Impairment in earning capacity Claimant's loss of ability to earn a living that has resulted from a work-related injury or occupational disease. Compensation awarded for impairment in earning capacity—which includes *Permanent total disability awards* and some awards for *Temporary partial disability*—has no inherent connection to actual loss of wages, even though claimant's wages at time of injury are used to compute the award and, in case of temporary-partial impairment in earning capacity awards, actual wage loss may be a presumptive basis for calculating weekly awards. See also *Compensation; Permanent total disability; Temporary partial disability.*

Impairment of wages See *Wage impairment.*

Incapacity See *Disability.*

Independent contractor An individual engaged by an entity (principal) to perform a job or a service but over whom the principal does not have the right to control the manner and means of performance. Independent contractors are not employees and, therefore, are generally not covered by workers' compensation.

Injury (1) Any physical or mental harm to an individual; (2) *Accident.*

Jurisdiction (1) The power of a government agency to act; (2) generic term for states, territories, commonwealths, the federal government, or other political entities.

Lost-time claim A claim for benefits that includes award of compensation for total or partial disability in addition to an award of medical benefits. See also *Medical-only claim.*

Medical impairment Loss of physical or mental functioning which is determined strictly on the basis of medical evidence, including but not limited to clinical tests, objective signs, and results of physical examination. See also *Disability.*

Medical-only claim A claim for benefits that includes only payments of bills for health-care providers. See also *Lost-time claim.*

Mental impairment See *Medical impairment.*

Minimal exposure rule Condition for coverage of certain occupational diseases by which claimants must establish that they had been subjected to injurious exposure for a specified period of time. Sometimes they must establish in-state exposure for specified period. See also *Occupational disease; Onset-of-disability rule.*

Noncomplying employer *Amenable employer* who has not complied with the workers' compensation law either by securing insurance coverage or by gaining approval to become a *Self-insuring employer*; usually liable for workers' compensation claims filed against its risk on dollar-for-dollar basis, and/or suable at common law without the common-law defenses of fellow-servant rule, assumption of risk, and contributory negligence, and/or subject to fines and/or criminal penalties.

Occupational disease An ailment that is contracted in the course of employment and is peculiar to an industrial trade or process in its causes, manifestations, frequency, or increased risk over that to which members of general public or of employments generally are exposed. Distinguished in most jurisdictions from *Injury* or *Accident*. See also *Change of occupation; Course of Employment; Minimal exposure rule; Onset-of-disability rule; Peculiar to industrial trade or process; Scheduled diseases.*

Onset-of-disability rule Condition of coverage for certain occupational diseases by which claimants are required to establish that disability or death ensued within a specified period of time from date of last injurious exposure. See also *Minimal exposure rule; Occupational disease.*

Peculiar to industrial trade or process A condition of coverage for *Occupational disease*, meaning that an employment exposes workers to a higher risk of contracting the disease than that to which the general public is exposed.

Permanent partial disability Disability caused by work-related injury or occupational disease that does not remove claimant from substantially remunerative employment but that has left the claimant with residual medical impairment that is expected to be of indefinite duration. See also *Scheduled-loss awards*.

Permanent total disability (1) Disability caused by work-related injury or occupational disease that completely removes claimant from substantially remunerative employment; (2) (in some jurisdictions) loss or loss of use of designated part or parts of the body, e.g., loss of both legs, loss of vision of both eyes.

Physical impairment See *Medical impairment*.

Recognized claim A claim that has been declared valid by the state or federal agency overseeing a workers' compensation system. See also *Certified claim*.

Safety-code (violation) claim Claim available in a limited number of jurisdictions for an additional award or penalty assessed against an employer whose violation of certain safety rules resulted in injury, occupational disease, or death.

Scheduled disease An *Occupational disease* that is listed on statutory schedule as associated with particular industrial trade or process and, therefore, presumptively caused by employment or presumptively *Peculiar to industrial trade or process*.

Scheduled-loss award Form of compensation for *Permanent partial disability* for loss or loss of use of body parts specified on statutory "schedule," usually awarded as a lump sum.

Second-injury fund Insurance fund, usually state-administered, under which costs or portions of costs of claims for aggravation of pre-existing conditions are paid rather than being charged to self-insured employer, employer's risk, or employer's insurance carrier.

Self-insuring employer Complying employer that has obtained the right (or privilege) to pay directly and, to some extent, administer claims filed by its employers, i.e., without obtaining private-insurance or state-fund coverage.

Settlement A formal agreement (usually requiring approval of state agency) by which all of the employer's or the insurer's liability under a claim is extinguished in exchange for a lump sum of money given to the claimant. See also *Stipulation*.

State fund Insurance fund administered by state or public entity; may be competitive, i.e., private insurance is permitted in jurisdiction, or monopolistic, i.e., private insurance is not permitted in jurisdiction.

Stipulation A formal agreement between parties to a claim (usually the claimant and employer) as to only certain specified issues in a claim. Usually requires approval of state agency. See also *Settlement*.

Substantially remunerative employment One of those intuitively derived terms for which no specific definition is helpful. Synonymous or descriptive phrases such as "gainful employment" or "earning power" appear, also intuitively, to be accurate or helpful, although they beg the definition. It appears clear that a worker who is capable of engaging in lighter or lower-paying work than that at which he or she was regularly engaged prior to the injury or occupational disease is still capable of substantially remunerative employment. On the other hand, the ability to engage in minimum activities from which some profit or wages might be derived does not necessarily mean that an individual is capable of engaging in substantially remunerative employment for workers' compensation purposes.

Temporary partial disability Disability caused by work-related injury or occupational disease that does not appear to be of indefinite duration and that is not keeping the claimant from gainful employment. Compensation awards for this disability include *Impairment in earning capacity awards* and *Wage-impairment awards*.

Temporary total disability (1) Disability caused by work-related injury or occupational disease that does not appear to be of indefinite duration but keeps the claimant from gainful employment; (2) Disability caused by work-related injury or occupational disease that keeps claimant from returning to regular employment. See also *Waiting period*.

Wage-impairment awards Temporary partial disability compensation awards that are designed to reimburse the claimant for actual loss or diminution of wages that resulted from a work-related injury or occupational disease.

Waiting period Short period of time—usually one week or less—after the injury or inception of occupational disease during which *Temporary total disability* is not payable unless lost time amounts to a specified period of time—usually between two and three consecutive weeks.

Work-relatedness General term for the causal connection that must be established by claimants between employment and disability. For *Occupational diseases*, usually expressed by saying that disease must be "contracted in course of employment" and "peculiar to industrial trade or process"; for injuries, by saying that injury must be "in course of and arising out of employment."

Selected Bibliography

GENERAL-UNITED STATES

The Bureau of National Affairs, Inc., Policy and Practice (series) includes up-to-date and useful digests of state and federal laws.

John Burton's Workers' Compensation Monitor is a periodical covering current issues and is published 10 times a year.

Larson, Workmen's Compensation Law (1952) (original ed., with updates) is the leading treatise in the field.

Malone, Plant & Little, Workers' Compensation and Employment Rights, Cases and Materials (2d ed. 1982), is an excellent casebook, both for its choice of cases and its commentary.

The Report of the National Commission on State Workmen's Compensation Laws (1972) and Compendium on Workmen's Compensation (1973) provide good summaries of the status of the U.S. compensation systems. Many of its charts and conclusions are still useful and the *Report's* recommendations remain valid.

U.S. Chamber of Commerce, Analysis of Workers' Compensation Laws (annual) provides a good, highly usable series of charts comparing the various U.S. and Canadian jurisdictions. Some of the charts are included in the appendix to this book.

FEDERAL

Norris, the Law of Maritime Personal Injuries, (3d ed. 1975, 2 vols. with supplements).

ALABAMA

Hood, Hardy & Saad, Alabama Workmen's Compensation (1984).

ARIZONA

Davis, Arizona Workers' Compensation (1980).

CALIFORNIA

California Continuing Education Bar, California Workers' Damages Practice (1985).

Hanna, Workers' Compensation Law of California (1985 with updates).

Herlick, California Workers' Compensation Law Handbook (3d ed. 1985, 2 vols.).

Swezey, California Workers' Compensation Practice (3d ed. 1985).

DISTRICT OF COLUMBIA

May, Workers' Compensation Practice Manual (2d ed. 1988).

FLORIDA

Alpert & Murphy, Florida Workmen's Compensation Law (3d ed. 1983, with annual bound supplements).

GEORGIA

Georgia Institute of Continuing Legal Education, Official Workers' Compensation Practice Manual (1984).

Hiers & Potter, Georgia Workers Compensation Law and Practice (1984).

Quillian, Workers' Compensation Claims: Attorney's Guide to Georgia W. Forms (1985).

IOWA

Hanssen, Iowa Legal Forms—Worker's Compensation (1983).

Lawyer & Higgs, Iowa Worker's Compensation Law & Practice (1984).

KENTUCKY

Champa, Kentucky Workers' Compensation (1982) (Harrison Company).

Harned, Kentucky Workers' Compensation (1984) (Lawyers' Cooperative Publishing Company).

MAINE

Devoe, Maine Workers' Compensation Act: Practice and Procedure (2d supp. 1985).

MARYLAND

Pressman, Workmen's Compensation in Maryland (2d ed. 1977, with 1980 supplement).

Singleton, Workmen's Compensation in Maryland (1935).

MASSACHUSETTS

MassCOSH Legal Committee, Injured on the Job: A Handbook for Massachusetts Workers, (Schwartz, ed.) (4th rev. ed. 1982).

MICHIGAN

Hunt, Workers' Compensation System in Michigan: A Closed Case Survey (1982).

MINNESOTA

Herbulock, A Guide to Minnesota Workers' Compensation (1982).

Peck, Minnesota Legal Forms: Workers' Compensation (1981).

Weber & Whisney, Minnesota Worker's Compensation: A Workbook for Business (1983).

MISSOURI

Kenter, Missouri Workers' Compensation (1984).

NEBRASKA

Cavel, Nebraska Legal Forms: Workmen's Compensation (1981).

NEW YORK

New York State Bar Association, Handling the Basic Workers' Compensation Case in New York (Magro, ed.) (1984).

NORTH CAROLINA

M. Anderson & Wake Forest University School of Law, North Carolina Workers' Compensation Manual (1983).

OHIO

Nackley, Ohio Workers' Compensation Claims (1982, with annual supplements).

Young, Ohio Workmen's Compensation (1972).

OKLAHOMA

Oldfield & Coker, Oklahoma Workers' Compensation (1985).

OREGON

Oregon State Bar Committee on Continuing Legal Education, Workers' Compensation.

PENNSYLVANIA

Barbieri, Pennsylvania Workmen's Compensation & Occupational Disease (1975, 3 vols).

TENNESSEE

Reynolds, Workers' Compensation, Practice & Procedure, With Forms (rev. ed.).

TEXAS

GAREY & MORRIS, HANDLING A WORKMEN'S COMPENSATION CLAIM (rev. ed.) (1975).

HARDBERGER, TEXAS WORKERS COMPENSATION TRIAL MANUAL (1984).

WASHINGTON

WASHINGTON BAR CONTINUING LEGAL EDUCATION, WORKERS' COMPENSATION UPDATE (1984).

Table of Cases

D

E

F

G

H

I

J

K

L

M

T

U

V

W

Y

Index

E

F

G

H

I

J

L

R

S

T

U

W

About the Author

Jeffrey V. Nackley has served as a staff hearing officer for the Ohio Industrial Commission and has practiced law extensively in the workers' compensation field. His publications on Ohio workers' compensation law have been cited by Ohio courts and other authorities. He is a member of the workers' compensation committee of the Ohio State Bar Association.

Mr. Nackley is also admitted to practice in the District of Columbia, where, in addition to engaging in private practice, he has served as a staff attorney for the Northern Mariana Islands Commission on Federal Laws. He has taught law school in the Washington, D.C., area and is currently a legal editor for The Bureau of National Affairs, Inc., *Labor Relations Reporter*.